5-INGREDIENT INSTANT POT COOKBOOK FOR TWO

5-Ingredient INSTANT POT COOKBOOK for Two

KIMBERLY SNEED

callisto publishing
an imprint of Sourcebooks

Published by Callisto Publishing LLC C/O Sourcebooks LLC

P.O. Box 4410, Naperville, Illinois 60567-4410

(630) 961-3900

callistopublishing.com

Printed and Bound In China

OGP 20

In memory of my father, Michael.
I know you would have been so proud.

Contents

Introduction

Welcome to the *5-Ingredient Instant Pot Cookbook for Two*. You may have noticed that there are a lot of Instant Pot cookbooks out there and countless Instant Pot recipes online. Often, these are for big families, larger portions, and fancy holiday meals—but not a lot for a party of two. So, if you're looking for perfectly portioned meals for you and your plus one, you've come to the right place. Or perhaps you just don't want to spend more money than necessary and don't want to deal with a lot of prep or leftovers—you're also in the right place. No matter the reason that brought you here, I am confident you will find recipes that you will love and want to come back to time and again.

As a huge fan of simple cooking, I have created numerous recipes over the years that have one major theme in mind: They're so easy that anyone can make them. I love food that is simple and straightforward but also full of flavor. Oh, and I love my Instant Pot. Perhaps like many of you, I owned one for months before actually using it. It can be a bit intimidating to begin with. However, with the explanations, tips and tricks, and easy 5-ingredient recipes you'll find in this cookbook, I guarantee that you'll get the hang of using it. And with every meal you make, you'll grow more comfortable.

I began to notice that I pulled out my Instant Pot only for dinner or big family meals, but with this book, I set out to change that. The Instant Pot is really an amazing appliance that can be used to make life easier in the kitchen every day. The recipes I've shared here are designed to help you get the most out of your Instant Pot—and, because each recipe requires no more than 5 main ingerdients, I know that you'll save time shopping, prepping, and cooking, too.

While working on the recipes for this cookbook, I fell in love with my Instant Pot all over again. I hope that the recipes in this book will help you take the first step toward using your Instant Pot, make the most of your Instant Pot, and, most of all, be more confident in creating delicious and easy meals with just a few ingredients.

Now let's get cooking!

Chicken Tacos, page 71

CHAPTER

INSTANT POT COOKING FOR TWO MADE SIMPLE

BEFORE WE GET TO THE RECIPES, I want to go over some Instant Pot basics as well as kitchen and shopping tips that will make it easier for you to create easy meals for two people using a maximum of 5 main ingredients.

UPGRADING YOUR KITCHEN ROUTINE

Ready to make your life easier in the kitchen? I'm right there with you! The Instant Pot is the perfect appliance to make an array of fresh, delicious meals for two that don't require a lot of prep or finishing. The Instant Pot is also the ultimate hands-off tool: The ingredients cook all together without requiring anyone to stand by the stove. Many recipes allow you to prep, then set it and forget it until it's piping hot and ready to serve! The Instant Pot also lends itself well to one-pot meals and other recipes that require less cleanup than traditional stovetop and oven-based cooking. I don't know about you but cleaning up after cooking is my nemesis. So, I love that once dinner is served, I only have to clean the inner pot and any prep surfaces and tools I may have used.

Because the Instant Pot is a wonderfully precise tool, it's also easier to cook smaller portions of food. Whether you're using a 3-quart ("Mini"), 6-quart, or 8-quart model, you can typically use the same methods, same ingredients, and same quantities to yield the same delicious results. Additionally, longer cooking processes like braising and roasting can be done in a fraction of the time. Don't worry if you forgot to take the chicken out of the freezer, because you can cook frozen meats in the Instant Pot, too! And because the Instant Pot recipes in this book all require only 5 or fewer ingredients, that's just one more way that you will save time and energy in the kitchen.

Recipes to Try Now

There are so many recipes here that I love to make on repeat. From breakfast to dessert, there are dishes that the Instant Pot does so well for two, that all use just 5 ingredients. Here are a few favorites to try first:

MUSHROOM RISOTTO (PAGE 54): Did you know it's a breeze to make creamy, restaurant-quality mushroom risotto right at home with the help of your Instant Pot? It's quick and easy—not to mention delicious.

HUMMUS (PAGE 39): Once you make homemade hummus, you'll never go back to store-bought! It's one of my favorite afternoon snacks, paired with pita chips. With this recipe you'll learn how to turn dry chickpeas into a creamy, garlicky dip for two.

CLASSIC POT ROAST (PAGE 92): Perfect for a big Sunday dinner, but for two! With this Instant Pot recipe, it's easy to get all the nostalgic taste of a weekend roast with a recipe that won't leave you with leftovers all week.

STEEL-CUT OATMEAL (PAGE 20): Breakfast is the most important meal of the day, right? And there's nothing like a bowl of warm, hearty oatmeal to kick things off. The Instant Pot makes it easy to whip this up.

CRÈME BRÛLÉE (PAGE 107): Ooh la la! Crème brûlée is my favorite dessert of all time, so using the Instant Pot to create it (and save time and effort) was at the top of my list. You must give this French delicacy a try.

WHY 5 INGREDIENTS?

Limiting a recipe to only 5 main ingredients not only makes the recipe easy, but it also allows the quality of those ingredients to shine. And because the Instant Pot is an electric pressure cooker, fewer nutrients leave the food during the cooking process than with other stovetop methods, making the food both healthier and more flavorful. The Instant Pot is the perfect appliance for 5-ingredient recipes—you can cook a variety of vegetables, grains, meats, and seafood to perfection without much added oil or fat.

The Instant Pot is also the ideal tool to build flavor, even with only 5 ingredients. For the purposes of this book, pantry staples such as water, salt, pepper, and oil/cooking spray are considered "freebie" ingredients. These essentials will help you build flavor and allow the main components of the dish to shine but are not counted in the ingredient lists. For instance, you can really add to the flavor of your meal by searing your meat in oil prior to pressure cooking, using the Sauté function. Additionally, sautéing vegetables and spices, such as onions and garlic, in oil beforehand can also enrich the flavors of your dish. Always be sure to deglaze the pan with water or broth after sautéing—the bits of food that stick to your inner pot are caramelized bits from what you have cooked that will add flavor to your meal as well as reduce the chances of a burn warning while pressure cooking in your Instant Pot.

Before we dive into recipes, let's cover the basics of Instant Pot use and 5-ingredient cooking.

GETTING TO KNOW THE INSTANT POT

There can be a bit of a learning curve when it comes to the Instant Pot, so before getting started, you'll want to familiarize yourself with the various parts, functions, and terminology—all of which I'll go over below. Don't worry; this will all become second nature once you start cooking through the recipes.

Parts

First up, there are a few parts to the Instant Pot that are different than other kitchen appliances or traditional pressure cookers you may have used that you'll want to get acquainted with.

LID: The Instant Pot lid twists to secure onto the pot for cooking. The lid features a handle, a lid position marker, a lid fin (which conveniently fits into the cooker handle as a handy lid-holder), a steam release handle, and a float valve.

STEAM RELEASE HANDLE: The steam release handle is the toggle that allows you to move between sealing and venting on the Instant Pot. In order to cook with pressure, the steam release handle must be set to sealing.

INNER POT: The inner pot is a removable stainless steel pot that is used for cooking in the Instant Pot.

FLOAT VALVE: The float valve on the Instant Pot is a pin lock mechanism that prevents the lid from accidentally being opened while there is a significant amount of pressure within the pot.

COOKER BASE: The Instant Pot cooker base is home to the heating element and houses the inner pot.

CONTROL PANEL: The control panel is where you will choose the cooking function as well as set the cook time.

HEATING ELEMENT: Underneath the inner pot in the cooker base is where you'll find the heating element. The control panel controls the heating element based on the cooking function and cook time you set.

Controls

The control panel of your Instant Pot is where you will set how you will cook your meals for two, including the cook function and time.

TIME DISPLAY: The time display indicates whether the Instant Pot is on or off, as well as the total cook time and remaining cook time.

PRESSURE INDICATOR: The pressure indicator specifies whether the Instant Pot is set to Low or High pressure.

COOKING PROGRAM KEYS: The cooking program keys on the Instant Pot are pre-programmed buttons for ease of use. The recipes in this cookbook will primarily use the Pressure Cook/Manual and Sauté buttons; however, most Instant Pot models have additional keys, such as Soup/Broth, Meat/Stew, Bean/Chili, Poultry, Rice, Multigrain, Porridge, Steam, Slow Cook, and Yogurt.

TIME-ADJUST KEYS: Once you choose a cooking program, you can use the time-adjust buttons (+) and (–) to increase or decrease the cook time.

OPERATION KEYS: The operation keys on the Instant Pot include Keep Warm and Cancel. The Keep Warm key turns the auto keep warm function on and off, and the Cancel key ends a cooking program at any time.

Key Terminology

Along with the different parts and controls, there are also a few Instant Pot–specific terms that you will want to be familiar with while using the appliance and cooking through the recipes in this cookbook.

NATURAL RELEASE is when you allow the cooker to cool down naturally after cooking with pressure. The time it takes the Instant Pot to cool will depend on the size and amount of food in your cooker. When the cooker is done cooling, the float valve will drop, allowing you to open the lid on the Instant Pot and access your food.

QUICK RELEASE is when you turn the steam release handle to venting to let the steam out from pressure cooking. Once all the steam is released, the float valve will drop, allowing you to open the lid on the Instant Pot and access your food.

POT-IN-POT COOKING is when you prepare your meal inside another oven-safe pot, pan, or accessory within the inner pot. This method is great for cooking meals you don't want to sit in liquid or ones that might burn in the inner pot, for desserts, and for cooking multiple items in the Instant Pot at the same time.

DEGLAZING is done after using the Sauté function to sear or cook ingredients, before pressure cooking begins. This process simply involves adding water or broth to the inner pot and scraping up any (yummy!) browned bits that might have accumulated on the inner pot during the sauté process.

INSTANT POT 101

SETTING THE COOKING FUNCTION: As mentioned, the Instant Pot has many functions, and those functions come with several buttons. For the purposes of this book, we're going to focus on the Pressure Cook button (sometimes labeled as "Manual," depending on which model you own), plus (+) and minus (–) buttons, and the Sauté button. Once you click the Pressure Cook button, you can add or reduce cook time using the plus (+) and minus (–) buttons. The Sauté button allows you to use the Instant Pot just like a sauté pan. You can brown and sear meats and precook vegetables to enhance the flavors of your Instant Pot meals.

SECURING THE LID: An important aspect of using the Instant Pot is knowing how to secure the lid and set the pressure valve. Holding the Instant Pot lid by its handle, put the lid on the cooker, aligning the mark on the lid with the open mark on the Instant Pot. Then rotate the lid clockwise until the mark on the lid is aligned with the close mark on the Instant Pot. You should hear a chime sound letting you know that it is properly closed.

NATURAL VERSUS QUICK RELEASE: An important feature of your Instant Pot is the steam release valve. To bring the Instant Pot up to pressure, the steam release valve must be set to sealing. Once the cook time is up, there are two ways that the pressure inside can be released. With natural pressure release, you simply leave the steam release valve in the sealing position and allow the pressure to reduce naturally over time. The amount of time is largely dependent on what and how much you are cooking. The second option is quick release (also known as manual pressure release). In this case, once the cook time is up, you will move the steam release handle to the venting position and let the remaining pressure escape as steam from the steam release valve. All of the recipes in this book will instruct you which release method to use, and you'll find that many recipes use a combination of the two methods (such as natural release for 20 minutes, followed by quick release).

CLEANING YOUR INSTANT POT: In order to maintain the quality of your Instant Pot and meals made in your Instant Pot, it is important to clean the appliance properly after each use. First, be sure to unplug the Instant Pot and allow the appliance to cool completely before cleaning. The inner pot can be cleaned with soap and water and is dishwasher safe. Wipe the lid and sealing valve clean with water, then dry with a cloth. Clean the Instant Pot itself with a damp cloth; do not submerge the cooker base in water.

Adjusting Recipes for High-Altitude Cooking

Did you know that water evaporates faster at higher altitudes? So, if you happen to live in the mountains or anywhere 2,000 feet above sea level, you're going to want to adjust your cooking times when using the Instant Pot.

Generally, recipe cooking times can be adjusted by 5 percent for every 1,000 feet of altitude above 2,000 feet. For instance, if you're cooking Chicken Tacos (page 71) at 3,000 feet, you'll want to increase the normal cook time of 15 minutes by 5 percent to approximately 16 minutes. Or if you're cooking a Classic Pot Roast (page 92) at 4,000 feet, you'll want to increase the normal cook time of 25 minutes by 10 percent to approximately 28 minutes.

TROUBLESHOOTING

While the Instant Pot is typically a reliable device, it's not completely foolproof, and mistakes can happen just like with any other appliance. Here are a few common issues that you might run into and how you can resolve them.

DIFFICULTY CLOSING THE LID: If you're having trouble closing the lid, be sure that the sealing ring is installed properly and that it isn't dirty or damaged.

DIFFICULTY OPENING THE LID: If you're having trouble opening the lid after the time is up on your meal, there is a chance that pressure still exists in the cooker. Use the steam release handle to quick-release the rest of the internal pressure and open the lid only after the pressure is completely released.

NOT COMING UP TO PRESSURE: The Instant Pot not sealing is one of the most common issues for new users. There are a few things you can check if the pot is not coming up to pressure properly. First, ensure that the sealing ring is properly installed, then check to see that the steam release valve is set to sealing and there is enough liquid to create steam and bring the Instant Pot to pressure. Also make sure the lid is closed properly.

LEAKING STEAM: It is normal for some steam to come out of the float valve while the Instant Pot is coming up to pressure. However, if steam continues to leak from the lid or elsewhere during the cooking process, there may be another issue. If steam is coming out of the sides, check to make sure the sealing ring is in place and is working properly (not dirty or damaged). If steam is leaking from the float valve after the pot has come up to pressure, you may have to clean or replace the silicone seal.

BURN WARNING: A "burn" message on your Instant Pot means that it is overheating and your food may begin to burn on the bottom of your inner pot. There are many ways that you can avoid this issue: Use enough liquid, allow your Instant Pot to cool after using the Sauté feature, deglaze the bottom of the inner pot after using the Sauté feature, and add starchy ingredients (such as pasta, rice, and tomato products) last and don't stir.

STOCKING THE 5-INGREDIENT KITCHEN

One of the things I love about the Instant Pot is that with just a few staple ingredients, you can make many delicious and affordable meals. There are quite a few staples that I use repeatedly in the recipes in this cookbook. If you have these ingredients on hand, you will always be able to throw together a quick and easy dinner with minimal effort and planning.

Refrigerator

- Milk
- Cheese
- Eggs
- Salsa (you can make some yourself with the recipe on page 119)
- Garlic (I like the ease of jarred minced garlic, but you can always use fresh garlic if you'd prefer.)
- Boneless, skinless chicken breasts
- Ground beef
- Canned biscuits

Freezer

- Broccoli
- Corn
- Peas and carrots
- Boneless, skinless chicken breasts
- Spinach

- Hash browns (I like O'Brien style with peppers and onions, but any type will work.)

Shelf Staples

- Olive oil
- Broth (I most often use chicken broth—learn how easy it is to make your own on page 116—and vegetable broth.)
- Evaporated milk (You can replace this with regular milk in most recipes.)
- Coconut milk (This is a great alternative for nondairy or vegan preferences.)
- Rice (Both white and brown rice are great to have on hand.)
- Canned and dried beans (I prefer red, pinto, and black beans.)
- Canned diced tomatoes (I like diced tomatoes with green peppers, celery, and onions.)
- Oatmeal (I prefer steel-cut oats, but you can also use quick oats.)
- Pasta (I always have spaghetti and penne on hand.)
- Potatoes
- Quinoa
- Cornstarch (This is great for thickening sauces.)

Spices

- Salt
- Black pepper
- Cajun seasoning
- Italian seasoning
- Chili powder
- Taco seasoning
- Ground cinnamon

Smart Shopping for Two

No need to shop until you drop! Here are some helpful shopping hints that will make the process of cooking for two even easier and more affordable. These tips will help you shop smaller, save money, and avoid food waste.

PURCHASE PRECISE AMOUNTS: Looking for a half-pound chuck roast for the Classic Pot Roast (page 92)? Instead of purchasing what is often sold in 1-pound increments and higher, head to your grocery store's butcher for a special cut and buy only what you need. This goes for the deli counter, too, where you can buy what you need in sliced meats and cheeses.

USE BULK BINS FOR EXACT PORTIONS: If your grocery store offers bulk options for staples like rice, dried beans, and more, they're not only great for buying large quantities but also perfect for pint-size portions. By buying only exactly what you need, you save money and avoid waste.

WRITE A GROCERY LIST: If you are trying to stay within a budget, it is helpful to plan your meals ahead of time. Make a list of all the items you need to buy for the week, and you'll find you're much less likely to over-spend at the grocery store.

SHOPPING SALES: Take advantage of sales on your big-ticket items, such as protein. Is chicken on sale? Then plan to make the Teriyaki Chicken (page 72) and Burrito Bowls with Chicken and Black Beans (page 78) this week. Sales are also a great time to stock up on staples like canned and frozen vegetables, pasta, and spices.

BUY WHAT'S IN SEASON: Buying what's in season means you get the freshest produce—and the prices are generally better, too!

EQUIPMENT ESSENTIALS

You can cook most things right in the inner pot of your Instant Pot. However, there are some Instant Pot accessories that will come in handy while cooking a few of the recipes in this cookbook.

SPRINGFORM PAN: A springform pan is a round pan with a side that is removable from the base. It's perfect for dishes you'd usually bake, like cheesecake.

BUNDT PAN: Known for its distinctive fluted doughnut shape, this pan is perfect for creating visually appealing desserts and breads, such as Monkey Bread (page 25).

SILICONE SLING: An essential tool for using pans safely in your Instant Pot, these slings can be used for lifting pans from your inner pot and for roasting meats, fish, vegetables, and more.

EGG BITE MOLD: Cook and store perfect portions in the same container. A silicone egg bite mold is perfect for making bite-size sous vide egg bites, muffins, and more.

RAMEKIN: Ramekins are perfect for presenting individual portions, such as soufflés and crème brûlée.

TIPS FOR COOKING WITH TWO PEOPLE IN THE KITCHEN

Too many cooks in the kitchen? Here are some best practices to follow to help streamline cooking with your plus one, making things even faster and easier.

DISCUSS WITH YOUR KITCHEN MATE HOW TO DIVIDE UP THE PREP. Does one person love to measure? Does the other hate chopping? Picking your preferred roles will help streamline the process and lead to a more enjoyable time in the kitchen.

DIVIDE COOKING AND CLEANUP. With these easy recipes, sometimes prep and cooking go hand in hand. With one person at the helm for preparing the meal, have another be the captain of cleanup!

TURN ON SOME TUNES. I don't know about you, but I'm always happier in the kitchen with my favorite playlist going. Put on something that you and your partner both enjoy, setting the mood for a delicious and easy dinner routine.

THE RECIPES IN THIS BOOK

There you have it! We've gone through several Instant Pot basics, parts, and terminology, as well as tips for shopping and cooking for two. The recipes that follow were designed to be easy enough to cook on a busy weeknight using any size or model of Instant Pot—and yield exactly two servings. Additionally, all the recipes can be made with no more than 5 ingredients (not including our "freebies" of water, salt, pepper, and oil/cooking spray).

To help you with meal prep and planning, I have also included labels indicating whether each recipe is "vegetarian" (meatless), a "one-pot meal" (a complete entrée where your protein plus grain or veggie are cooked together in the Instant Pot), "quick" (can be made in 30 minutes or less from start to finish), or "worth the wait" (takes longer than 45 minutes, including come-to-pressure and release time).

I'm excited for you to start cooking! I hope that these recipes help you get the most from your Instant Pot, save money, reduce waste, and have some fun in the kitchen—all while preparing delicious meals. Enjoy your 2-person, 5-ingredient cooking journey!

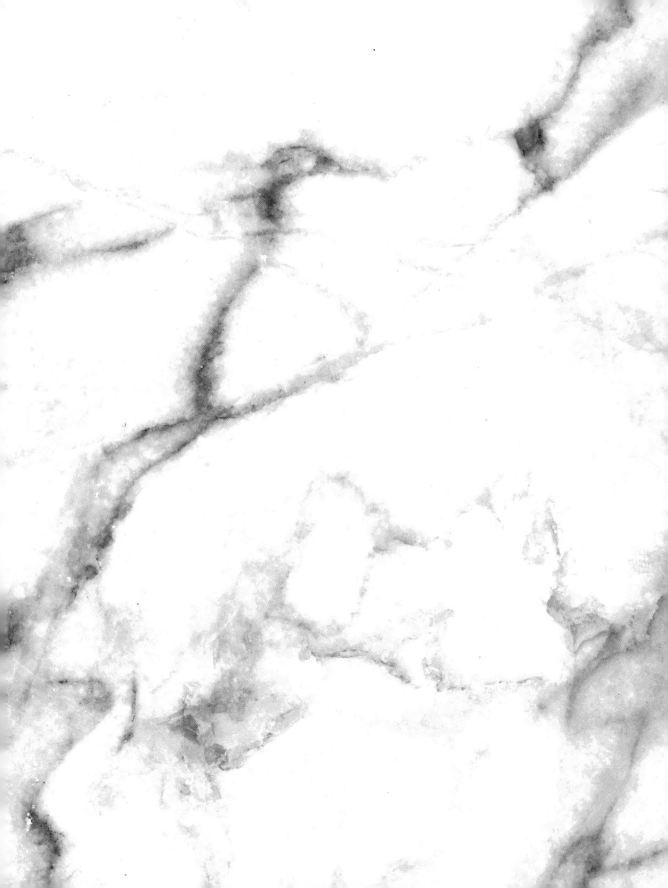

CHAPTER

BREAKFAST AND BRUNCH

CHEESY EGG BITES

Serves 2

PREP & FINISHING: 10 minutes   **PRESSURE COOK:** 10 minutes on High
PRESSURE RELEASE: Natural for 5 minutes, then Quick   **TOTAL TIME:** 30 minutes

Skip the coffeehouse egg bites and make your own from the comfort of home. The Instant Pot makes easy work of your favorite sous vide–style egg bites for a fraction of the cost.

Nonstick cooking spray	¼ teaspoon salt	¼ chopped frozen broccoli florets
3 large eggs	¼ teaspoon black pepper	⅓ cup shredded cheese, divided
2 tablespoons milk		

1. Spray the 7 cavities of an egg bite mold with cooking spray.

2. In a small bowl, whisk together the eggs, milk, salt, and pepper.

3. Add the frozen broccoli and half of the cheese, and stir to combine.

4. Evenly pour or spoon the egg mixture into the prepared egg bite mold and top with the remaining cheese. Cover with the egg bite mold lid.

5. Place a trivet in the bottom of the Instant Pot, then pour in 1½ cups water. Place the filled egg bite mold on the trivet.

6. Lock the lid in place. Select Pressure Cook and adjust the pressure to High and the time to 10 minutes. After cooking, let the pressure release naturally for 5 minutes, then quick release any remaining pressure.

7. Once the float valve drops, open the lid and carefully remove the mold from the Instant Pot.

8. Let the egg bites cool for 5 minutes before removing from the mold. Serve warm.

VARIATION TIP: Feel free to change up the vegetables or the type of cheese, or add chopped cooked ham or bacon.

Per Serving: Calories: 197; Carbohydrates: 2g; Fat: 14g; Fiber: 0g; Protein: 15g; Sugar: 1g; Sodium: 528mg

MUFFIN BITES

Serves 2

PREP & FINISHING: 5 minutes   **PRESSURE COOK:** 12 minutes on High
PRESSURE RELEASE: Natural for 5 minutes, then Quick   **TOTAL TIME:** 27 minutes

These mini muffin bites are sure to satisfy cravings on a busy morning.

Nonstick cooking spray

½ large ripe banana

1 large egg, beaten

2 tablespoons
peanut butter

¼ cup steel-cut oats

1 tablespoon agave
syrup or honey (optional)

½ teaspoon
baking powder

⅛ teaspoon salt

1. Spray the 7 cavities of an egg bite mold with cooking spray.

2. In a small bowl, mash the banana until it is smooth.

3. Add the egg, peanut butter, oats, agave syrup (if using), baking powder, and salt and stir until well combined.

4. Evenly pour or spoon the muffin mixture into the prepared egg bite mold, then cover with the egg bite mold lid.

5. Place a trivet in the bottom of the Instant Pot, then pour in 1½ cups water. Place the filled egg bite mold on the trivet.

6. Lock the lid in place. Select Pressure Cook and adjust the pressure to High and the time to 12 minutes. After cooking, let the pressure release naturally for 5 minutes, then quick release any remaining pressure.

7. Once the float valve drops, open the lid and carefully remove the mold from the Instant Pot.

8. Let the muffin bites cool for 5 minutes before removing from the mold. Serve warm.

VARIATION TIP: Try topping each muffin bite with a bit of chopped fruit, nuts, or even mini chocolate chips in step 4, before closing the lid.

Per Serving: Calories: 239; Carbohydrates: 25g; Fat: 12g; Fiber: 4g; Protein: 10g; Sugar: 6g; Sodium: 350mg

Breakfast and Brunch

PANCAKE BITES

Serves 2

PREP & FINISHING: 10 minutes **PRESSURE COOK:** 10 minutes on High
PRESSURE RELEASE: Natural for 5 minutes, then Quick **TOTAL TIME:** 30 minutes

Love pancakes but don't love standing at the griddle? Whip up a batch of these perfectly portioned bites for an easy pancake breakfast.

Nonstick cooking spray

½ cup all-purpose flour

1 tablespoon sugar

½ teaspoon baking powder

⅛ teaspoon salt

1 tablespoon beaten egg

½ cup milk

Maple syrup, for serving (optional)

1. Spray the 7 cavities of an egg bite mold with cooking spray.

2. In a small bowl, whisk together the flour, sugar, baking powder, and salt.

3. Add the egg and milk and stir to combine.

4. Evenly pour or spoon the pancake batter into the prepared egg bite mold, then cover with the egg bite mold lid.

5. Place a trivet in the bottom of the Instant Pot, then pour in 1½ cups water. Place the filled egg bite mold on the trivet.

6. Lock the lid in place. Select Pressure Cook and adjust the pressure to High and the time to 10 minutes. After cooking, let the pressure release naturally for 5 minutes, then quick release any remaining pressure.

7. Once the float valve drops, open the lid and carefully remove the mold from the Instant Pot.

8. Let the pancake bites cool for 5 minutes before removing from the mold. Serve warm, topped with maple syrup if desired.

VARIATION TIP: Try adding mini chocolate chips or blueberries to your pancake batter!

Per Serving: Calories: 213; Carbohydrates: 33g; Fat: 5g; Fiber: 1g; Protein: 8g; Sugar: 9g; Sodium: 308mg

SPINACH AND FETA FRITTATA

Serves 2

PREP & FINISHING: 5 minutes   **PRESSURE COOK:** 15 minutes on High
PRESSURE RELEASE: Natural for 5 minutes, then Quick   **TOTAL TIME:** 30 minutes

You don't need to heat up the stove or oven for this convenient frittata—all the cooking is done right in the Instant Pot.

Nonstick cooking spray

4 large eggs

2 teaspoons milk
or cream

¼ teaspoon salt

⅛ teaspoon
black pepper

1 cup fresh spinach

¼ cup crumbled
feta cheese

1. Spray a 6- or 7-inch round pan (whatever fits best in your Instant Pot) with cooking spray.

2. In a small bowl, whisk together the eggs, milk, salt, and pepper. Add the feta cheese and stir to combine.

3. Put the spinach in the prepared pan, then pour the egg mixture over the spinach. Cover tightly with aluminum foil.

4. Place a trivet in the bottom of the Instant Pot, then pour in 1½ cups water. Place the pan on the trivet.

5. Lock the lid in place. Select Pressure Cook and adjust the pressure to High and the time to 15 minutes. After cooking, let the pressure release naturally for 5 minutes, then quick release any remaining pressure.

6. Once the float valve drops, open the lid and carefully remove the pan from the Instant Pot.

7. Slice the frittata into 4 pieces and serve warm.

USE IT UP: Store leftovers, tightly covered, in the refrigerator for up to 3 days. To serve, break up the frittata with a fork, wrap in a tortilla, and warm up for an easy breakfast burrito.

Per Serving: Calories: 200; Carbohydrates: 2g; Fat: 14g; Fiber: 0g; Protein: 16g; Sugar: 1g; Sodium: 614mg

Breakfast and Brunch

STEEL-CUT OATMEAL

Serves 2

PREP & FINISHING: 5 minutes   **PRESSURE COOK:** 2 minutes on High
PRESSURE RELEASE: Natural for 5 minutes, then Quick   **TOTAL TIME:** 17 minutes

Start your day off right with a hearty bowl of steel-cut oatmeal, cooked to perfection in the Instant Pot. I love to top mine with seasonal fruit and a little brown sugar.

Nonstick cooking spray

1 cup steel-cut oats

1½ cups water

1 cup nondairy milk (such as almond or oat milk)

⅛ teaspoon salt

Brown sugar, chopped fresh fruit, and/or nuts, for topping (optional)

1. Spray the bottom of the Instant Pot with cooking spray.

2. Add the oats, water, nondairy milk, and salt and stir to combine.

3. Lock the lid in place. Select Pressure Cook and adjust the pressure to High and the time to 2 minutes. After cooking, let the pressure release naturally for 5 minutes, then quick release any remaining pressure.

4. Once the float valve drops, open the lid and stir the oatmeal.

5. Serve warm with your favorite toppings.

VARIATION TIP: Make it savory. Top your oatmeal with a fried egg, sliced tomatoes, and shredded cheese for a different take on this breakfast bowl. Also, if your Instant Pot has a Porridge smart key, give it a try. By default, the button cooks at high pressure for different lengths of time. Press the button and adjust the time as noted above.

Per Serving: Calories: 390; Carbohydrates: 66g; Fat: 7g; Fiber: 11g; Protein: 14g; Sugar: 5g; Sodium: 215mg

FRENCH TOAST CASSEROLE

Serves 2

PREP & FINISHING: 10 minutes   **PRESSURE COOK:** 25 minutes on High
PRESSURE RELEASE: Natural for 5 minutes, then Quick   **TOTAL TIME:** 45 minutes

Skip the multiple steps and mess of traditional French toast and make this delicious and easy small-batch version in the Instant Pot.

Nonstick cooking spray

1 large egg

1 cup milk

¼ cup plus 1 tablespoon packed light brown sugar, divided

½ teaspoon ground cinnamon

3 cups sourdough bread cubes

Maple syrup, for topping (optional)

1. Spray a 6- or 7-inch round pan (whatever fits best in your Instant Pot) with cooking spray.

2. In a small bowl, whisk together the egg, milk, ¼ cup of brown sugar, and cinnamon.

3. Scatter the bread cubes in the prepared pan and cover with the egg mixture. Let this set for 5 minutes to allow the bread to soak up the egg mixture.

4. Sprinkle the remaining 1 tablespoon of brown sugar on top of the bread. Cover the pan tightly with aluminum foil.

5. Place a trivet in the bottom of the Instant Pot, then pour in 1½ cups water. Place the pan on the trivet.

6. Lock the lid in place. Select Pressure Cook and adjust the pressure to High and the time to 25 minutes. After cooking, let the pressure release naturally for 5 minutes, then quick release any remaining pressure.

7. Once the float valve drops, open the lid and carefully remove the pan from the Instant Pot.

8. Serve warm with maple syrup, if you like.

SUBSTITUTION TIP: Use your favorite nondairy milk instead.

Per Serving: Calories: 622; Carbohydrates: 112g; Fat: 10g; Fiber: 3g; Protein: 22g; Sugar: 46g; Sodium: 536mg

Breakfast and Brunch

21

BREAKFAST BURRITOS

Serves 2

PREP & FINISHING: 5 minutes   **PRESSURE COOK:** 25 minutes on High
PRESSURE RELEASE: Natural for 5 minutes, then Quick   **TOTAL TIME:** 40 minutes

Need an ample but easy breakfast on the go? There's nothing better than a warm and filling breakfast burrito to start your day right.

Nonstick cooking spray

4 large eggs

¼ cup shredded cheddar cheese

¼ teaspoon salt

⅛ teaspoon black pepper

¾ cup frozen potatoes O'Brien (with onions and peppers)

⅓ cup chopped ham

2 burrito-size flour tortillas

1. Spray a 6- or 7-inch round pan (whatever fits best in your Instant Pot) with cooking spray.

2. In a small bowl, whisk together the eggs, cheese, salt, and pepper.

3. Scatter the frozen potatoes in the bottom of the prepared pan. Top with the ham.

4. Pour the egg mixture on top. Cover the pan tightly with aluminum foil.

5. Place a trivet in the bottom of the Instant Pot, then pour in 1½ cups water. Place the pan on the trivet.

6. Lock the lid in place. Select Pressure Cook and adjust the pressure to High and the time to 25 minutes. After cooking, let the pressure release naturally for 5 minutes, then quick release any remaining pressure.

7. Once the float valve drops, open the lid and carefully remove the pan from the Instant Pot.

8. Stir to combine, then spoon into tortillas, roll up, and serve warm.

SUBSTITUTION TIP: Replace the diced ham with your favorite chopped vegetables to make this a great vegetarian breakfast option.

Per Serving: Calories: 511; Carbohydrates: 51g; Fat: 21g; Fiber: 3g; Protein: 28g; Sugar: 3g; Sodium: 971mg

SAUSAGE AND EGG CASSEROLE

Serves 2

PREP & FINISHING: 5 minutes   **SAUTÉ:** 5 minutes   **PRESSURE COOK:** 20 minutes on High
PRESSURE RELEASE: Natural for 5 minutes, then Quick   **TOTAL TIME:** 35 minutes

Who doesn't love a good casserole? With the Instant Pot it's easy to make a smaller casserole for two. This one is made with eggs, potatoes, and sausage, and you won't have to worry about leftovers.

Nonstick cooking spray

1 tablespoon olive oil

8 ounces loose breakfast sausage

4 large eggs

¼ cup milk

½ cup shredded cheddar cheese

½ teaspoon salt

¼ teaspoon black pepper

1 cup frozen potatoes O'Brien (with onions and peppers)

1. Spray a 6- or 7-inch round pan (whatever fits best in your Instant Pot) with cooking spray.

2. Set the Instant Pot to Sauté and pour in the olive oil.

3. Once the oil is shimmering, add the breakfast sausage. Cook the sausage, stirring to break up the meat, until cooked through, 4 to 5 minutes. Once cooked, press Cancel to turn off the Instant Pot.

4. Transfer the sausage to a plate and wipe out the inner pot with paper towels.

5. In a small bowl, whisk together the eggs, milk, cheese, salt, and pepper.

6. Scatter the frozen potatoes in the bottom of the prepared pan. Top with the sausage.

7. Pour the egg mixture on top of the potatoes and sausage. Cover the pan tightly with aluminum foil.

8. Place a trivet in the bottom of the Instant Pot, then pour in 1½ cups water. Place the pan on the trivet.

continued

Breakfast and Brunch

23

9. Lock the lid in place. Select Pressure Cook and adjust the pressure to High and the time to 15 minutes. After cooking, let the pressure release naturally for 5 minutes, then quick release any remaining pressure.

10. Once the float valve drops, open the lid and carefully remove the pan from the Instant Pot.

11. Slice the casserole into 4 pieces and serve warm.

SUBSTITUTION TIP: Swap out the breakfast sausage for your favorite vegetables to make this dish vegetarian.

Per Serving: Calories: 801; Carbohydrates: 19g; Fat: 62g; Fiber: 1g; Protein: 39g; Sugar: 3g; Sodium: 1,231mg

MONKEY BREAD

Serves 2

PREP & FINISHING: 15 minutes   **PRESSURE COOK:** 20 minutes on High
PRESSURE RELEASE: Quick   **TOTAL TIME:** 40 minutes

You can never go wrong with a decadent monkey bread recipe. There's something simple and delicious about biscuits, cinnamon, and sugar.

Nonstick cooking spray	¼ teaspoon ground cinnamon	2 tablespoons butter, melted
3 tablespoons granulated sugar	1 (7.5-ounce) container canned biscuits	¼ cup packed light brown sugar

1. Spray a 3-cup Bundt pan (or other nonstick round pan) with cooking spray.

2. In a small bowl, mix the granulated sugar and cinnamon together.

3. Open the can of biscuits and cut each biscuit into four pieces.

4. Dunk each piece into the cinnamon-sugar mixture and roll to coat. Place in the prepared pan.

5. In a small bowl, stir together the melted butter and brown sugar. Drizzle the mixture over the biscuit pieces. Cover the pan tightly with aluminum foil.

6. Place a trivet in the bottom of the Instant Pot, then pour in 1½ cups water. Place the pan on the trivet.

7. Lock the lid in place. Select Pressure Cook and adjust the pressure to High and the time to 20 minutes. After cooking, move the steam release handle to venting and quick release the pressure.

8. Once the float valve drops, open the lid and carefully remove the pan from the Instant Pot.

9. Let the pan sit for 10 minutes, then invert onto a plate. Serve warm.

Per Serving: Calories: 607; Carbohydrates: 95g; Fat: 23g; Fiber: 1g; Protein: 7g; Sugar: 53g; Sodium: 839mg

Breakfast and Brunch

BANANA BREAD

Serves 2

PREP & FINISHING: 5 minutes   **PRESSURE COOK:** 45 minutes on High
PRESSURE RELEASE: Natural for 5 minutes, then Quick   **TOTAL TIME:** 1 hour

Once you make banana bread in the Instant Pot, you'll never want to go back. This recipe makes a perfect portion for 2 for breakfast or an afternoon snack.

Nonstick cooking spray

1 ripe banana

⅓ teaspoon baking soda

Pinch salt

⅓ cup sugar

1 large egg, beaten

½ cup all-purpose flour

1. Spray a 6- or 7-inch round pan (whatever fits best in your Instant Pot) with cooking spray.

2. In a small bowl, mash the banana until smooth.

3. Add the baking soda and salt and stir to combine. Add the sugar and egg and stir to combine. Add the flour and stir to combine.

4. Pour the batter into the prepared pan, cover with a paper towel, then cover the pan tightly with aluminum foil.

5. Place a trivet in the bottom of the Instant Pot, then pour in 1½ cups water. Place the pan on the trivet.

6. Lock the lid in place. Select Pressure Cook and adjust the pressure to High and the time to 45 minutes. After cooking, let the pressure release naturally for 5 minutes, then quick release any remaining pressure.

7. Once the float valve drops, open the lid and carefully remove the pan from the Instant Pot.

8. Slice into 4 pieces and serve warm.

VARIATION TIP: Stir in chopped pecans for a banana-nut bread.

Per Serving: Calories: 331; Carbohydrates: 70g; Fat: 3g; Fiber: 2g; Protein: 7g; Sugar: 40g; Sodium: 320mg

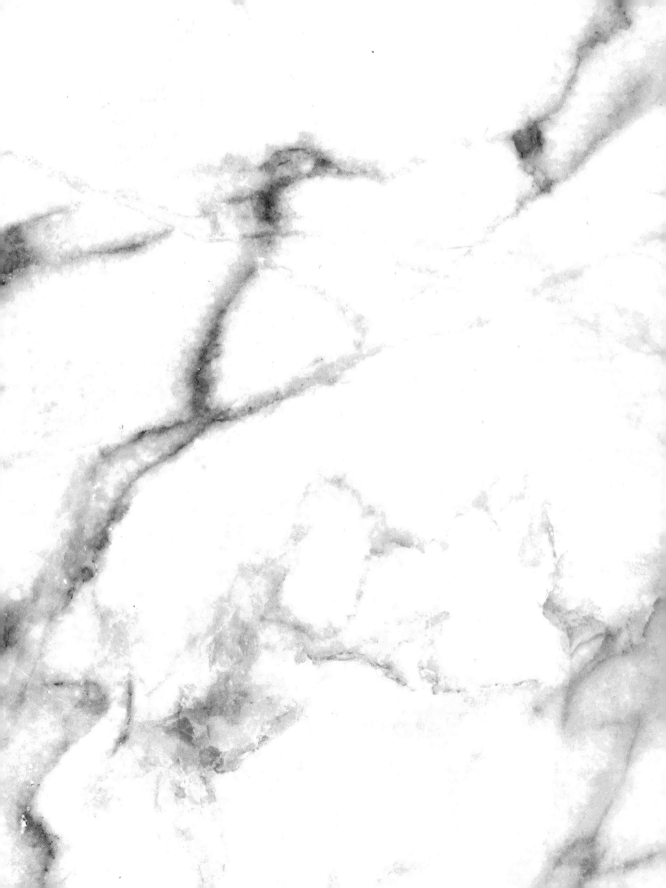

CHAPTER

SNACKS AND SIDES

BRUSSELS SPROUTS

Serves 2

PREP & FINISHING: 10 minutes   **PRESSURE COOK:** 1 minute on Low
PRESSURE RELEASE: Quick   **TOTAL TIME:** 16 minutes

If you think you don't like Brussels sprouts, you probably haven't had them prepared properly. The Instant Pot is a great way to cook them to perfection! Red pepper flakes spice things up a bit, and Parmesan adds another layer of flavor.

¾ cup vegetable broth

8 Brussels sprouts, halved

1 tablespoon olive oil

1 teaspoon minced garlic

½ teaspoon salt

⅛ teaspoon black pepper

Pinch red pepper flakes

½ cup grated Parmesan cheese

1. Place a trivet in the bottom of the Instant Pot, then pour in the broth.

2. Put the Brussels sprouts on top of the trivet, drizzle with the olive oil, and sprinkle with the garlic, salt, black pepper, and red pepper flakes.

3. Lock the lid in place. Select Pressure Cook and adjust the pressure to Low and the time to 1 minute. After cooking, move the steam release handle to venting and quick release the pressure.

4. Once the float valve drops, open the lid and carefully remove the Brussels sprouts.

5. Toss the Brussels sprouts with the Parmesan cheese and serve warm.

VARIATION TIP: Swap the Parmesan for crumbled feta cheese to change things up or add crumbled cooked bacon for more protein.

Per Serving: Calories: 199; Carbohydrates: 11g; Fat: 14g; Fiber: 3g; Protein: 10g; Sugar: 2g; Sodium: 932mg

MASHED POTATOES

Serves 2

PREP & FINISHING: 10 minutes   **PRESSURE COOK:** 8 minutes on High
PRESSURE RELEASE: Quick   **TOTAL TIME:** 23 minutes

Mashed potatoes are a great side to serve with so many different types of main courses. The Instant Pot makes easy work of this classic dish, especially for a party of two. With this recipe you don't have to worry about having a big pot of leftovers, but you still get all the flavor of creamy, homemade mashed potatoes.

1 pound russet potatoes (2 medium potatoes), peeled and sliced

½ teaspoon salt, plus more to taste

4 tablespoons butter

2 tablespoons sour cream

2 tablespoons milk

½ teaspoon black pepper

1. Combine the sliced potatoes and salt in the Instant Pot, then pour in 1 cup water.

2. Lock the lid in place. Select Pressure Cook and adjust the pressure to High and the time to 8 minutes. After cooking, move the steam release handle to venting and quick release the pressure.

3. Once the float valve drops, open the lid and press Cancel to turn off the Instant Pot.

4. Drain the potatoes, then return them to the inner pot.

5. Add the butter, sour cream, and milk to the potatoes and use a potato masher or immersion blender to mash until smooth.

6. Season with salt and pepper and serve warm.

SUBSTITUTION TIP: Don't have sour cream on hand? Substitute 2 tablespoons cream cheese for an equally creamy result.

Per Serving: Calories: 415; Carbohydrates: 42g; Fat: 26g; Fiber: 3g; Protein: 6g; Sugar: 3g; Sodium: 787mg

BAKED POTATOES

Serves 2

PREP & FINISHING: 5 minutes   **PRESSURE COOK:** 14 minutes on High
PRESSURE RELEASE: Natural for 20 minutes, then Quick   **TOTAL TIME:** 44 minutes

Baked potatoes are a great side for grilled steak or chicken, and they're so simple to make in the Instant Pot. Try topping your baked potato with some Barbecue Pulled Pork (page 88), steamed vegetables, and shredded cheese for a complete meal.

1 pound russet potatoes (2 medium potatoes), well scrubbed

2 tablespoons butter

½ teaspoon salt

¼ teaspoon black pepper

1. Place a trivet in the bottom of the Instant Pot, then pour in 1 cup water.

2. Pierce the potatoes with a fork on all sides and place them on top of the trivet.

3. Lock the lid in place. Select Pressure Cook and adjust the pressure to High and the time to 14 minutes. After cooking, let the pressure release naturally for 20 minutes, then quick release any remaining pressure.

4. Once the float valve drops, open the lid and carefully remove the potatoes.

5. Cut each potato in half lengthwise, top with butter, and season with salt and pepper.

VARIATION TIP: Top your baked potatoes with sour cream, snipped chives, shredded cheese, sliced scallions, and crumbled cooked bacon for classic loaded baked potatoes.

Per Serving: Calories: 281; Carbohydrates: 41g; Fat: 12g; Fiber: 3g; Protein: 5g; Sugar: 1g; Sodium: 684mg

POTATO SALAD

Serves 2

PREP & FINISHING: 15 minutes   **PRESSURE COOK:** 5 minutes on High
PRESSURE RELEASE: Quick   **TOTAL TIME:** 25 minutes

You don't need a big potluck to prepare your favorite barbecue side dishes. This is perfectly portioned so you can enjoy homemade potato salad anytime.

1 pound russet potatoes (2 medium potatoes), peeled and chopped

2 large eggs

⅓ cup mayonnaise

1 tablespoon yellow mustard

1 pickle, chopped, plus splash of pickle juice

½ teaspoon salt

¼ teaspoon black pepper

1. Put the potatoes in the Instant Pot. Place the whole eggs on top of the potatoes. Pour in 1 cup water.

2. Lock the lid in place. Select Pressure Cook and adjust the pressure to High and the time to 5 minutes. After cooking, move the steam release handle to venting and quick release the pressure.

3. Once the float valve drops, open the lid and transfer the eggs to a bowl of ice-cold water. Drain the potatoes and transfer to a bowl.

4. Once cool, peel the eggs and slice in half lengthwise. Put the yolks in a small bowl.

5. Add the mayonnaise, mustard, pickle juice, salt, and pepper to the yolks and mash with a fork until it becomes a smooth dressing.

6. Pour the dressing over the warm potatoes. Chop the egg whites and add them to the potatoes, along with the chopped pickle.

7. Stir well, cover, and refrigerate until ready to serve.

VARIATION TIP: Add a stalk of celery, diced, for more flavor and texture.

Per Serving: Calories: 510; Carbohydrates: 44g; Fat: 33g; Fiber: 4g; Protein: 12g; Sugar: 3g; Sodium: 1,526mg

Snacks and Sides

DEVILED EGGS

Serves 2

PREP & FINISHING: 10 minutes   **PRESSURE COOK:** 5 minutes on High
PRESSURE RELEASE: Natural for 5 minutes, then Quick   **TOTAL TIME:** 25 minutes

Cure that craving for deviled eggs in under 30 minutes with your Instant Pot! This iconic finger food is a breeze to make.

4 large eggs

2 tablespoons mayonnaise

½ teaspoon Dijon mustard

½ teaspoon pickle juice

¼ teaspoon salt

⅛ teaspoon black pepper

⅛ teaspoon paprika

1. Place a trivet in the Instant Pot, then pour in 1 cup water. Place the eggs on the trivet.

2. Lock the lid in place. Select Pressure Cook and adjust the pressure to High and the time to 5 minutes.

3. After cooking, let the pressure release naturally for 5 minutes, then quick release any remaining pressure.

4. Once the float valve drops, open the lid and transfer the eggs to a bowl of ice-cold water.

5. Once cool, peel the eggs and slice in half lengthwise. Put the yolks in a small bowl.

6. Add the mayonnaise, mustard, pickle juice, salt, and pepper to the yolks and mash with a fork until smooth.

7. Transfer the filling to a small zip-top plastic bag and seal. Cut one corner off the bag and pipe the filling into the egg white halves. (Alternatively, you can use a piping bag with a star tip.)

8. Sprinkle with the paprika and refrigerate until ready to serve.

VARIATION TIP: Add bacon bits and crumbled blue cheese to take your deviled eggs to the next level!

Per Serving: Calories: 240; Carbohydrates: 1g; Fat: 20g; Fiber: 0g; Protein: 13g; Sugar: 1g; Sodium: 545mg

CORN ON THE COB

Serves 2

PREP & FINISHING: 5 minutes   **PRESSURE COOK:** 2 minutes on High
PRESSURE RELEASE: Quick   **TOTAL TIME:** 12 minutes

There is nothing that says summer better than fresh corn on the cob. It's the perfect side for grilled meats, adding a crunchy sweetness to any meal. And it's foolproof to make in the convenience of the Instant Pot.

2 ears corn, husks and silk removed	2 tablespoons butter

1. Place a trivet in the bottom of the Instant Pot, then pour in 1 cup water.

2. Place the ears of corn on the trivet.

3. Lock the lid in place. Select Pressure Cook and adjust the pressure to High and the time to 2 minutes. After cooking, move the steam release handle to venting and quick release the pressure.

4. Once the float valve drops, open the lid and carefully remove the corn. Pour out the water from the inner pot.

5. Return the inner pot to the Instant Pot and add the butter, letting it melt from the residual heat.

6. Pour the melted butter over the corn and serve warm.

VARIATION TIP: Top your corn with some mayonnaise, chili powder, crumbled cotija cheese, and fresh cilantro leaves for delicious street corn.

Per Serving: Calories: 225; Carbohydrates: 27g; Fat: 13g; Fiber: 4g; Protein: 4g; Sugar: 5g; Sodium: 113mg

Snacks and Sides

GLAZED CARROTS

Serves 2

PREP & FINISHING: 5 minutes **SAUTÉ:** 5 minutes **PRESSURE COOK:** 10 minutes on High
PRESSURE RELEASE: Quick **TOTAL TIME:** 20 minutes

Looking for a new side dish to try? If you love glazed carrots during the holidays, this recipe will have you creating a small-batch version to enjoy any night of the year. The brown sugar and cinnamon pair with the carrots for a side dish you'll truly enjoy.

2 cups baby carrots

2 tablespoons butter

2 tablespoons packed light brown sugar

¼ teaspoon ground cinnamon

¼ teaspoon salt

¾ cup water, divided

1 tablespoon cornstarch

1. Combine the carrots, butter, brown sugar, cinnamon, and salt in the Instant Pot. Pour in ½ cup of water.

2. Lock the lid in place. Select Pressure Cook and adjust the pressure to High and the time to 10 minutes. After cooking, move the steam release handle to venting and quick release the pressure.

3. Once the float valve drops, open the lid. Press Cancel to turn off the Instant Pot, then set the Instant Pot to Sauté.

4. In a small bowl, whisk together the cornstarch and remaining ¼ cup water until completely dissolved. Pour the cornstarch slurry into the Instant Pot while whisking the glaze.

5. Allow to cook for 4 to 5 minutes, stirring occasionally, until the glaze has thickened. Press Cancel to turn off the Instant Pot. Serve carrots warm.

SUBSTITUTION TIP: Out of brown sugar? You can easily substitute the same amount of honey or maple syrup for a similarly sweet result.

Per Serving: Calories: 220; Carbohydrates: 29g; Fat: 12g; Fiber: 4g; Protein: 1g; Sugar: 19g; Sodium: 470mg

CILANTRO AND LIME RICE

Serves 2

PREP & FINISHING: 5 minutes   **PRESSURE COOK:** 3 minutes on High
PRESSURE RELEASE: Natural for 10 minutes, then Quick   **TOTAL TIME:** 23 minutes

Skip the takeout line and make this cilantro-lime rice for Veggie Burritos (page 62), Burrito Bowls with Chicken and Black Beans (page 78), and more from the comfort of your kitchen. The lime juice and chopped cilantro add flavor and dimension to traditional white rice and will brighten any meal.

1 cup vegetable broth	½ teaspoon salt	1 tablespoon lime juice
½ tablespoon grated lime zest	¾ cup white rice	2 tablespoons chopped fresh cilantro

1. Combine the broth, lime zest, and salt in the Instant Pot and stir. Add the rice, pushing it down into the broth.

2. Lock the lid in place. Select Pressure Cook and adjust the pressure to High and the time to 3 minutes. After cooking, let the pressure release naturally for 10 minutes, then quick release any remaining pressure.

3. Once the float valve drops, open the lid, fluff the rice with a fork, and stir in the lime juice and cilantro. Serve warm.

> **USE IT UP:** Have leftovers? Store in an airtight container in the refrigerator for up to 4 days. Pair leftover rice with chicken and beans wrapped up in a warm tortilla for a flavorful burrito.

Per Serving: Calories: 265; Carbohydrates: 59g; Fat: 0g; Fiber: 1g; Protein: 5g; Sugar: 0g; Sodium: 583mg

Snacks and Sides

SPANISH RICE

Serves 2

PREP & FINISHING: 5 minutes   **SAUTÉ:** 2 minutes   **PRESSURE COOK:** 4 minutes on High
PRESSURE RELEASE: Natural for 10 minutes, then Quick   **TOTAL TIME:** 26 minutes

Spanish rice is the perfect side for tacos, enchiladas, and more! With this recipe, white rice is cooked in tomato sauce and spices for a zesty side that will complement a variety of dishes. And with this small-batch recipe, you can make it for any meal without worrying about the leftovers.

1 tablespoon olive oil	1 cup vegetable broth	½ cup tomato sauce
¾ cup white rice	½ teaspoon chili powder	1 tablespoon chopped fresh cilantro (optional)
2 teaspoons minced garlic	½ teaspoon salt	

1. Set the Instant Pot to Sauté and add the olive oil.

2. Once the oil is shimmering, add the rice and garlic, and sauté for 1 minute. Press Cancel to turn off the Instant Pot.

3. Pour in the broth and scrape up any brown bits from the bottom of the pot.

4. Add the chili powder, salt, and tomato sauce and stir, making sure the rice is completely covered.

5. Lock the lid in place. Select Pressure Cook and adjust the pressure to High and the time to 4 minutes. After cooking, let the pressure release naturally for 10 minutes, then quick release any remaining pressure.

6. Once the float valve drops, open the lid, fluff the rice with a fork, and stir in the chopped cilantro (if using).

VARIATION TIP: Add ½ cup frozen peas and carrots at the beginning of the cooking process for added flavor and texture.

Per Serving: Calories: 344; Carbohydrates: 63g; Fat: 7g; Fiber: 2g; Protein: 6g; Sugar: 2g; Sodium: 893mg

HUMMUS

Serves 2

PREP & FINISHING: 15 minutes   **PRESSURE COOK:** 35 minutes on High
PRESSURE RELEASE: Natural for 20 minutes, then Quick   **TOTAL TIME:** 1 hour 15 minutes

With this homemade hummus recipe, you'll learn how to turn dry chickpeas into a creamy, garlicky dip for two.

½ cup dried chickpeas

1½ cups water

2 tablespoons tahini

1 tablespoon minced garlic

2 tablespoons lemon juice

2 tablespoons olive oil, plus more for drizzling

½ teaspoon cumin

½ teaspoon salt

Paprika (optional)

1. Combine the chickpeas and water in the Instant Pot.

2. Lock the lid in place. Select Pressure Cook and adjust the pressure to High and the time to 35 minutes. After cooking, let the pressure release naturally for 20 minutes, then quick release any remaining pressure.

3. Once the float valve drops, open the lid, reserve ½ cup of the chickpea cooking water, then drain the rest of the water from the beans.

4. Combine the tahini, garlic, and lemon juice in a blender and blend until smooth.

5. Add the chickpeas, olive oil, cumin, salt, and 1 tablespoon of the reserved cooking water to the blender and blend until smooth.

6. Continue to add tablespoons of the reserved cooking water until the desired consistency is reached.

7. To serve, spoon the hummus into a bowl, drizzle with additional olive oil, and sprinkle with paprika (if using).

VARIATION TIP: Add a few jarred roasted red peppers during the blending process for a zesty take on classic hummus.

Per Serving: Calories: 409; Carbohydrates: 37g; Fat: 25g; Fiber: 8g; Protein: 13g; Sugar: 6g; Sodium: 613mg

Snacks and Sides

CHAPTER

SOUPS AND STEWS

SPRING PEA AND MINT SOUP

Serves 2

PREP & FINISHING: 10 minutes   **SAUTÉ:** 5 minutes   **PRESSURE COOK:** 4 minutes on High
PRESSURE RELEASE: Natural for 5 minutes, then Quick   **TOTAL TIME:** 29 minutes

This simple spring soup can be served warm on chilly nights or chilled on sunny days. Packed full of veggie protein, it's a great vegetarian option for a light weeknight meal.

1 tablespoon olive oil	2 cups frozen green peas	¼ teaspoon salt
½ onion, chopped	¼ cup fresh mint leaves	⅛ teaspoon black pepper
2 teaspoons minced garlic	2½ cups vegetable broth	

1. Set the Instant Pot to Sauté and add the olive oil.

2. Once the oil is shimmering, add the onion and sauté for 2 to 3 minutes, until slightly translucent.

3. Add the garlic and continue to sauté for 1 minute. Press Cancel to turn off the Instant Pot.

4. Add the peas, mint leaves, vegetable broth, salt and pepper, and stir.

5. Lock the lid in place. Select Pressure Cook and adjust the pressure to High and the time to 4 minutes. After cooking, let the pressure release naturally for 5 minutes, then quick release any remaining pressure.

6. Once the float valve drops, open the lid. Using an immersion blender, blend the soup well. Serve hot or chilled.

VARIATION TIP: This soup tastes great with even more veggies! Try adding carrots, celery, or kale along with the peas for added flavor and nutrients. You can also garnish your soup with some fresh mint and parsley leaves.

Per Serving: Calories: 183; Carbohydrates: 23g; Fat: 7g; Fiber: 7g; Protein: 8g; Sugar: 8g; Sodium: 441mg

CLASSIC CHILI

Serves 2

PREP & FINISHING: 5 minutes   **SAUTÉ:** 5 minutes   **PRESSURE COOK:** 10 minutes on High
PRESSURE RELEASE: Natural for 5 minutes, then Quick   **TOTAL TIME:** 30 minutes

Chili is a great meal for cooler months or game day, and this recipe whips up a batch for two. Serve with corn bread or with your favorite corn chips for dipping.

1 tablespoon olive oil

8 ounces lean ground beef

¼ teaspoon salt

⅛ teaspoon black pepper

1 cup water

1½ tablespoons chili seasoning (half a 1.25-ounce packet)

1 (15-ounce) can mixed chili beans

1 (14.5-ounce) can diced tomatoes with onion, celery, and green pepper

1 (8-ounce) can tomato sauce

1. Set the Instant Pot to Sauté and pour in the olive oil.

2. Once the oil is shimmering, add the ground beef and season with the salt and pepper. Cook, stirring to break up the meat, until cooked through, about 5 minutes. Press Cancel to turn off the Instant Pot.

3. Pour in the water and scrape up any browned bits from the bottom of the pot.

4. Add the chili seasoning and beans with their juices and stir. Add the tomatoes with their juices, then pour the tomato sauce on top; do not stir.

5. Lock the lid in place. Select Pressure Cook and adjust the pressure to High and the time to 10 minutes. After cooking, let the pressure release naturally for 5 minutes, then quick release any remaining pressure.

6. Once the float valve drops, open the lid and stir the chili. Serve warm with your favorite toppings.

VARIATION TIP: Going easy on red meat? You can swap in an equal amount of ground turkey or chicken.

Per Serving: Calories: 528; Carbohydrates: 52g; Fat: 20g; Fiber: 18g; Protein: 37g; Sugar: 5g; Sodium: 1,532mg

Soups and Stews

CHICKEN TORTILLA SOUP

Serves 2

PREP & FINISHING: 5 minutes   **PRESSURE COOK:** 12 minutes on High
PRESSURE RELEASE: Natural for 5 minutes, then Quick   **TOTAL TIME:** 27 minutes

Quick and flavorful, this chicken tortilla soup is perfect for serving on a chilly night. Top with tortilla strips for a restaurant-quality dish made with the convenience of the Instant Pot.

1 (15-ounce) can seasoned black beans

½ cup frozen corn kernels

½ cup salsa (store-bought or homemade, page 119)

1 (5- to 6-ounce) boneless, skinless chicken breast

1 cup chicken broth (store-bought or homemade, page 116)

Crunchy tortilla strips, for serving (optional)

1. Combine the black beans with their juices, corn, and salsa in the Instant Pot.

2. Put the chicken on top of the beans and corn. Cover with the broth, but don't stir.

3. Lock the lid in place. Select Pressure Cook and adjust the pressure to High and the time to 12 minutes. After cooking, let the pressure release naturally for 5 minutes, then quick release any remaining pressure.

4. Once the float valve drops, open the lid and transfer the chicken to a plate or cutting board.

5. Shred the chicken with two forks, then return the meat to the soup and stir it in.

6. Serve warm with crunchy tortilla strips, if using.

VARIATION TIP: Add a dash of heavy cream and some shredded cheddar cheese for a flavorful, creamy tortilla soup.

Per Serving: Calories: 332; Carbohydrates: 44g; Fat: 3g; Fiber: 13g; Protein: 33g; Sugar: 4g; Sodium: 519mg

MINESTRONE

Serves 2

PREP & FINISHING: 5 minutes   **PRESSURE COOK:** 2 minutes on High
PRESSURE RELEASE: Natural for 5 minutes, then Quick   **TOTAL TIME:** 17 minutes

This veggie-packed Italian soup always takes me back to childhood! It's easy to make a small batch of this classic recipe with just a few ingredients and the convenience of the Instant Pot.

½ cup frozen mixed vegetables

1 (15-ounce) can kidney beans

1 (14.5-ounce) can diced tomatoes with onion, celery, and green pepper

1 cup vegetable broth

½ cup small shell pasta

Grated Parmesan cheese, for serving (optional)

1. Combine the frozen vegetables, kidney beans with their juices, diced tomatoes with their juices, vegetable broth, and pasta in the Instant Pot and stir.

2. Lock the lid in place. Select Pressure Cook and adjust the pressure to High and the time to 2 minutes. After cooking, let the pressure release naturally for 5 minutes, then quick release any remaining pressure.

3. Once the float valve drops, open the lid and stir.

4. Serve warm, topped with Parmesan cheese, if you like.

SUBSTITUTION TIP: Swap the kidney beans for cannellini beans, or the pasta for an equal amount of white or brown rice for a slightly bulkier and more textured take on this classic soup.

Per Serving: Calories: 326; Carbohydrates: 63g; Fat: 1g; Fiber: 11g; Protein: 18g; Sugar: 3g; Sodium: 843mg

Soups and Stews

JAMBALAYA

Serves 2

PREP & FINISHING: 15 minutes   **SAUTÉ:** 5 minutes   **PRESSURE COOK:** 8 minutes on High
PRESSURE RELEASE: Natural for 5 minutes, then Quick   **TOTAL TIME:** 38 minutes

Get a taste of the Big Easy with this simple yet hearty jambalaya recipe.

6 ounces smoked sausage, sliced

1 cup water

1 cup white rice

1 tablespoon Cajun seasoning

1 (14.5-ounce) can diced tomatoes with onion, celery, and green pepper

10 medium raw shrimp, peeled and deveined

Louisiana hot sauce, for serving (optional)

1. Set the Instant Pot to Sauté and, once warm, put the sliced sausage in the Instant Pot.

2. Sauté the sausage until cooked through, about 5 minutes. Press Cancel to turn off the Instant Pot. Transfer the cooked sausage to a plate.

3. Pour the water into the Instant Pot and scrape up any brown bits from the bottom of the pot.

4. Add the rice and Cajun seasoning and stir. Top with the diced tomatoes with their juices, but do not stir.

5. Lock the lid in place. Select Pressure Cook and adjust the pressure to High and the time to 8 minutes. After cooking, let the pressure release naturally for 5 minutes, then quick release any remaining pressure.

6. Once the float valve drops, open the lid and stir, then add the shrimp and reserved sausage. Replace the Instant Pot lid and allow the ingredients to heat through for 5 minutes in the residual heat.

7. Serve warm with hot sauce, if desired.

VARIATION TIP: Add chicken to kick this meal up a notch. Cut a boneless, skinless chicken breast into 1-inch pieces and sauté just after cooking the smoked sausage, then let it cook along with the rice and Cajun seasoning.

Per Serving: Calories: 672; Carbohydrates: 86g; Fat: 25g; Fiber: 1g; Protein: 22g; Sugar: 0g; Sodium: 1,261mg

BEEF STEW

Serves 2

PREP & FINISHING: 15 minutes   **SAUTÉ:** 10 minutes
PRESSURE COOK: 35 minutes on High   **PRESSURE RELEASE:** Natural for 5 minutes, then Quick
TOTAL TIME: 1 hour 10 minutes

There's nothing better on a chilly winter night than a hearty bowl of beef stew. This recipe combines seasoned stew meat with vegetables for a warm, savory dish, rich in flavor.

1 tablespoon olive oil

8 ounces beef stew meat, cubed

¼ teaspoon salt

⅛ teaspoon black pepper

1 cup water

1 cup peeled and cubed russet potatoes

1 carrot, cut into ½-inch pieces

1 celery stalk, cut into ½-inch pieces

1½ tablespoons beef stew seasoning (half a 1.25-ounce packet)

1. Set the Instant Pot to Sauté and pour in the olive oil.

2. Once the oil is shimmering, add the beef stew meat and season with the salt and pepper. Cook until browned on all sides, about 10 minutes, then press Cancel to turn off the Instant Pot.

3. Pour in the water and scrape up any browned bits from the bottom of the pot.

4. Add the potatoes, carrot, and celery, and stew seasoning, and stir to combine.

5. Lock the lid in place. Select Pressure Cook and adjust the pressure to High and the time to 35 minutes. After cooking, let the pressure release naturally for 5 minutes, then quick release any remaining pressure.

6. Once the float valve drops, open the lid and stir the stew. Serve warm.

SUBSTITUTION TIP: Switch up the veggies! This stew is also great with sliced mushrooms, diced white onion, diced bell pepper, and more.

Per Serving: Calories: 287; Carbohydrates: 19g; Fat: 12g; Fiber: 2g; Protein: 27g; Sugar: 3g; Sodium: 452mg

Soups and Stews

CHICKEN AND DUMPLINGS

Serves 2

PREP & FINISHING: 10 minutes **SAUTÉ:** 10 minutes **PRESSURE COOK:** 3 minutes on High
PRESSURE RELEASE: Natural for 10 minutes, then Quick **TOTAL TIME:** 38 minutes

With just a few ingredients and minimal prep work, you'll be enjoying a hot bowl of savory chicken and fluffy dumplings in no time.

1 tablespoon olive oil

1 (5- to 6-ounce) boneless, skinless chicken breast, cut into 1-inch pieces

1½ cups chicken broth (store-bought or home-made, page 116)

½ cup frozen peas and carrots

¼ teaspoon salt

¼ teaspoon black pepper

1 (7.5-ounce) can biscuits, cut into 1-inch pieces

¼ cup heavy cream

1. Set the Instant Pot to Sauté and pour in the olive oil.

2. Once the oil is shimmering, add chicken and cook until browned on all sides, about 10 minutes. Press Cancel to turn off the Instant Pot.

3. Pour in the broth and scrape up any browned bits from the bottom of the pot.

4. Add the peas and carrots, salt, and pepper, and stir to combine. Top with the biscuit pieces.

5. Lock the lid in place. Select Pressure Cook and adjust the pressure to High and the time to 3 minutes. After cooking, let the pressure release naturally for 10 minutes, then quick release any remaining pressure.

6. Once the float valve drops, open the lid, add the heavy cream, stir, and heat to simmering.

7. Serve warm.

SUBSTITUTION TIP: Have a favorite homemade biscuit recipe? Skip the refrigerated ones for dollops of your biscuit dough.

Per Serving: Calories: 625; Carbohydrates: 57g; Fat: 31g; Fiber: 4g; Protein: 28g; Sugar: 11g; Sodium: 1,147mg

CHEESY POTATO SOUP

Serves 2

PREP & FINISHING: 5 minutes **PRESSURE COOK:** 10 minutes on High
PRESSURE RELEASE: Natural for 15 minutes, then Quick **TOTAL TIME:** 35 minutes

It's easy to make a small-batch version of this restaurant-favorite soup with a few pantry staples, most of which you probably already have. You'll come back to this flavorful soup recipe time and again.

2 cups frozen potatoes O'Brien (with onions and peppers)

1½ cups chicken broth (store-bought or home-made, page 116)

1 tablespoon all-purpose flour

¼ cup milk

¼ teaspoon salt

⅛ teaspoon black pepper

2 cups shredded cheddar cheese

Sliced scallions, for serving (optional)

Crumbled cooked bacon, for serving (optional)

1. Combine the potatoes and broth in the Instant Pot.

2. Lock the lid in place. Select Pressure Cook and adjust the pressure to High and the time to 10 minutes. After cooking, let the pressure release naturally for 15 minutes, then quick release any remaining pressure. Press Cancel to turn off the Instant Pot.

3. Meanwhile, in a small bowl, whisk together the flour, milk, salt, and pepper.

4. Once the float valve drops, open the lid, add the flour mixture and cheese, and stir until the cheese is melted.

5. Serve the soup warm, topped with scallions and bacon, if using.

SUBSTITUTION TIP: You can use fresh russet potatoes instead of the frozen ones; sub in 2 potatoes, peeled and chopped, plus some chopped onion for flavor.

Per Serving: Calories: 634; Carbohydrates: 37g; Fat: 39g; Fiber: 2g; Protein: 33g; Sugar: 3g; Sodium: 1,077mg

Soups and Stews

CHICKEN NOODLE SOUP

Serves 2

PREP & FINISHING: 10 minutes   **PRESSURE COOK:** 10 minutes on High
PRESSURE RELEASE: Quick   **SAUTÉ:** 5 minutes   **TOTAL TIME:** 30 minutes

This small-batch soup recipe is the perfect cozy pick-me-up on those chillier days or for when you want a lighter meal. Skip the canned stuff, which can be full of sodium.

2 carrots, peeled and cut into ¼-inch pieces

2 celery stalks, chopped

1 (5- to 6-ounce) boneless, skinless chicken breast

2 cups chicken broth (store-bought or home-made, page 116)

1 cup egg noodles

½ teaspoon salt

¼ teaspoon black pepper

1. Combine the carrots and celery in the Instant Pot. Place the chicken on top of the vegetables and cover with the broth. Do not stir.

2. Lock the lid in place. Select Pressure Cook and adjust the pressure to High and the time to 10 minutes. After cooking, move the steam release handle to venting and quick release the pressure. Press Cancel to turn off the Instant Pot.

3. Once the float valve drops, open the lid and transfer the chicken to a plate. Set the Instant Pot to Sauté.

4. Once the soup begins to boil, add the egg noodles and allow to simmer for 5 minutes, or until tender.

5. Shred the chicken with two forks, then return the meat to the soup and stir it in.

6. Season with the salt and pepper and serve warm.

VARIATION TIP: Add a dash of heavy cream for a bowl of creamy chicken soup.

Per Serving: Calories: 197; Carbohydrates: 20g; Fat: 2g; Fiber: 3g; Protein: 22g; Sugar: 4g; Sodium: 703mg

ROASTED RED PEPPER AND TOMATO SOUP

Serves 2

PREP & FINISHING: 5 minutes   **SAUTÉ:** 2 minutes   **PRESSURE COOK:** 7 minutes on High
PRESSURE RELEASE: Natural for 5 minutes, then Quick   **TOTAL TIME:** 24 minutes

This soup is the perfect pairing for a grilled cheese sandwich. The addition of roasted red pepper makes for a tasty alternative to canned soup.

1 tablespoon olive oil

2 teaspoons minced garlic

1 cup vegetable broth

1 (14.5-ounce) can diced tomatoes with onion, celery, and green pepper

½ cup jarred roasted red peppers, drained

½ cup milk

¼ teaspoon black pepper

1. Set the Instant Pot to Sauté and pour in the olive oil.

2. Once the oil is shimmering, add the minced garlic and sauté for 1 minute, or until fragrant. Press Cancel to turn off the Instant Pot.

3. Pour in the broth and scrape up any bits from the bottom of the pot.

4. Add the diced tomatoes with their juices and the red peppers and stir.

5. Lock the lid in place. Select Pressure Cook and adjust the pressure to High and the time to 7 minutes. After cooking, let the pressure release naturally for 5 minutes, then quick release any remaining pressure.

6. Once the float valve drops, open the lid, add the milk, and blend the soup with an immersion blender until smooth.

7. Season with pepper and serve warm.

VARIATION TIP: Looking for a creamier and more decadent soup? Swap out the milk for ¼ cup heavy cream.

Per Serving: Calories: 138; Carbohydrates: 13g; Fat: 9g; Fiber: 1g; Protein: 4g; Sugar: 5g; Sodium: 752mg

Soups and Stews

CHAPTER

MEATLESS MAINS

MUSHROOM RISOTTO

Serves 2

PREP & FINISHING: 5 minutes **SAUTÉ:** 5 minutes **PRESSURE COOK:** 6 minutes on High
PRESSURE RELEASE: Quick **TOTAL TIME:** 21 minutes

Serve up restaurant-quality risotto from the comfort of your home! It's so easy to cook in the Instant Pot—it turns out delicious and creamy every time.

1 tablespoon olive oil

¼ cup chopped onion

½ cup chopped cremini mushrooms

1½ cups vegetable broth

¾ cup arborio rice

¼ teaspoon salt

⅛ teaspoon black pepper

¼ cup shredded Parmesan

Chopped fresh parsley or chives, for serving (optional)

1. Set the Instant Pot to Sauté and pour in the olive oil.

2. Once the oil is shimmering, add the onion and mushrooms and cook, stirring often, until the onions are translucent, 3 to 4 minutes. Press Cancel to turn off the Instant Pot.

3. Stir in the broth, rice, salt, and pepper and scrape up any brown bits from the bottom of the pot.

4. Lock the lid in place. Select Pressure Cook and adjust the pressure to High and the time to 6 minutes. After cooking, move the steam release handle to venting and quick release the pressure.

5. Once the float valve drops, open the lid and stir in the Parmesan until heated through.

6. Serve immediately, topped with chopped parsley or chives, if desired.

> **SUBSTITUTION TIP:** Skip the Parmesan for a delicious dairy-free risotto.
> **USE IT UP:** Have leftover mushrooms? To make them last longer, remove from their packaging, wrap in paper towels, and store in an open plastic bag in the refrigerator.

Per Serving: Calories: 381; Carbohydrates: 61g; Fat: 10g; Fiber: 3g; Protein: 9g; Sugar: 1g; Sodium: 523mg

RED BEANS AND RICE

Serves 2

PREP & FINISHING: 5 minutes   **PRESSURE COOK:** 25 minutes on High
PRESSURE RELEASE: Natural for 10 minutes, then Quick   **TOTAL TIME:** 45 minutes

Bring the taste of New Orleans home with this simple beans and rice recipe. Skip the premade mixes and make a nourishing meal for two using only a few simple pantry staples.

¾ cup white rice

¾ cup dried red beans

2 teaspoons Cajun seasoning

3 cups vegetable broth

½ cup salsa (store-bought or homemade, page 119)

1. Combine the rice, beans, Cajun seasoning, and vegetable broth in the Instant Pot and stir.

2. Top with the salsa, but do not stir.

3. Lock the lid in place. Select Pressure Cook and adjust the pressure to High and the time to 25 minutes. After cooking, let the pressure release naturally for 10 minutes, then quick release any remaining pressure.

4. Once the float valve drops, open the lid and stir to mix. Serve warm.

VARIATION TIP: Try adding sliced smoked andouille sausage. You can cook the sausage in the Instant Pot using the Sauté feature and set aside, then stir into the beans and rice just before serving.

Per Serving: Calories: 515; Carbohydrates: 107g; Fat: 1g; Fiber: 13g; Protein: 21g; Sugar: 4g; Sodium: 467mg

Meatless Mains

MAC AND CHEESE

Serves 2

PREP & FINISHING: 5 minutes   **PRESSURE COOK:** 4 minutes on High
PRESSURE RELEASE: Quick   **TOTAL TIME:** 14 minutes

That iconic blue box has nothing on this creamy homemade mac and cheese. The blend of cheeses adds a level of complexity to this quick and easy Instant Pot meal.

2 cups elbow macaroni

2 cups water

3 tablespoons butter

½ teaspoon salt

½ cup whole milk

2 cups shredded sharp cheddar cheese

1 cup grated Parmesan cheese

1. Combine the elbow macaroni, water, butter, and salt in the Instant Pot and stir.

2. Lock the lid in place. Select Pressure Cook and adjust the pressure to High and the time to 4 minutes. After cooking, move the steam release handle to venting and quick release the pressure.

3. Once the float valve drops, open the lid and give the macaroni a good stir. Press Cancel to turn off the Instant Pot.

4. Add the milk, followed by the cheddar and Parmesan cheeses by the handful. Continue stirring until the cheese is completely melted. Serve warm.

VARIATION TIP: Try a different cheese, such as Gruyère, for a completely different flavor profile.

Per Serving: Calories: 1,248; Carbohydrates: 90g; Fat: 73g; Fiber: 3g; Protein: 57g; Sugar: 6g; Sodium: 2,181mg

VEGETABLE CURRY

Serves 2

PREP & FINISHING: 10 minutes **PRESSURE COOK:** 5 minutes on High
PRESSURE RELEASE: Quick **TOTAL TIME:** 20 minutes

Who needs takeout when you can make a curry this easily? Plus, with servings for just two people, you can be sure you won't be dealing with endless leftovers. Add your favorite vegetables to bring your own spin to this delicious vegetarian dish.

1 sweet potato, peeled and cubed

1 (15-ounce) can chickpeas, rinsed and drained

1 (14.5-ounce) can diced tomatoes with onion, celery, and green pepper

1 (14-ounce) can light coconut milk

1 cup water, divided

2 teaspoons red curry paste

Cooked rice, for serving (optional)

Plain yogurt, for serving (optional)

1. Combine the sweet potato, chickpeas, diced tomatoes with their juices, coconut milk, and ½ cup of water in the Instant Pot and stir.

2. In a small bowl, whisk the curry paste into the remaining ½ cup of water. Pour the curry mixture on top of the vegetables, but do not stir.

3. Lock the lid in place. Select Pressure Cook and adjust the pressure to High and the time to 5 minutes. After cooking, move the steam release handle to venting and quick release the pressure.

4. Once the float valve drops, open the lid and stir. Serve warm over rice and top with a spoonful of yogurt, if desired.

VARIATION TIP: For a little variety, try using different vegetables that are currently in season, like butternut squash or pumpkin in autumn.

Per Serving: Calories: 502; Carbohydrates: 51g; Fat: 30g; Fiber: 10g; Protein: 13g; Sugar: 7g; Sodium: 912mg

Meatless Mains

QUINOA STUFFED PEPPERS

Serves 2

PREP & FINISHING: 10 minutes   **PRESSURE COOK:** 11 minutes on High
PRESSURE RELEASE: Natural for 15 minutes, then Quick   **TOTAL TIME:** 47 minutes

The Instant Pot makes easy work of what would otherwise be a complex dish.

1 (15-ounce) can black beans, rinsed and drained

¾ cup water

¼ cup quinoa

¼ cup salsa (store-bought or homemade, page 119)

¼ teaspoon salt

⅛ teaspoon black pepper

2 large bell peppers (any color)

¼ cup shredded cheese

1. Combine the black beans, water, quinoa, salsa, salt, and pepper in the Instant Pot and stir.

2. Lock the lid in place. Select Pressure Cook and adjust the pressure to High and the time to 1 minute. After cooking, let the pressure release naturally for 5 minutes, then quick release any remaining pressure.

3. Once the float valve drops, open the lid and stir.

4. Slice the tops off the bell peppers and remove the seeds and ribs. Spoon half of the quinoa mixture into each bell pepper.

5. Wipe out the inner pot. Place a trivet in the bottom, then pour in 1½ cups water.

6. Carefully stand the peppers on top of the trivet (if necessary, use a ramekin or aluminum foil to help them stay upright).

7. Lock the lid in place. Select Pressure Cook and adjust the pressure to High and the time to 10 minutes. After cooking, move the steam release handle to venting and quick release the pressure.

8. Once the float valve drops, open the lid, sprinkle the cheese on top of the peppers, and replace the lid for a minute to allow the cheese to melt.

9. Open the lid, carefully remove the peppers, and serve warm.

Per Serving: Calories: 366; Carbohydrates: 56g; Fat: 7g; Fiber: 17g; Protein: 20g; Sugar: 8g; Sodium: 620mg

PENNE ALLA VODKA

Serves 2

PREP & FINISHING: 5 minutes   **SAUTÉ:** 8 minutes   **PRESSURE COOK:** 4 minutes on High
PRESSURE RELEASE: Quick   **TOTAL TIME:** 22 minutes

Time to step up your spaghetti night with this creamy and delicious pasta dish. The classic flavors of penne alla vodka come together in just a few steps.

1 tablespoon olive oil	2 cups penne pasta	¼ cup heavy cream
¼ cup chopped onion	2 teaspoons salt	¼ teaspoon black pepper
¼ cup vodka	1 (14.5-ounce) can diced tomatoes	¼ cup grated Parmesan cheese (optional)
2 cups water		

1. Set the Instant Pot to Sauté and pour in the olive oil.

2. Once the oil is shimmering, add the onion and cook until translucent, 3 to 4 minutes.

3. Pour in the vodka and cook until reduced by half, 3 to 4 minutes. Press Cancel to turn off the Instant Pot.

4. Stir in the water, penne, and salt. Pour the diced tomatoes with their juices over the penne, but do not stir.

5. Lock the lid in place. Select Pressure Cook and adjust the pressure to High and the time to 4 minutes. After cooking, move the steam release handle to venting and quick release the pressure.

6. Once the float valve drops, open the lid and stir in the cream. Let stand for 3 minutes.

7. Stir in the pepper and top with Parmesan cheese, if using.

VARIATION TIP: The flavors in this dish work well with pancetta. Dice it up and sauté with the onion for a delicious variation on this classic Italian dish.

Per Serving: Calories: 657; Carbohydrates: 88g; Fat: 20g; Fiber: 8g; Protein: 16g; Sugar: 10g; Sodium: 2,581mg

Meatless Mains

PAD THAI

Serves 2

PREP & FINISHING: 5 minutes   **SAUTÉ:** 5 minutes   **PRESSURE COOK:** 5 minutes on High
PRESSURE RELEASE: Quick   **TOTAL TIME:** 20 minutes

Skip takeout tonight and instead try this easy-to-make noodle dish. I love the mix of textures and flavors from the noodles, bean sprouts, egg, and peanuts.

2 tablespoons olive oil, divided

1 large egg, lightly beaten

¼ cup pad thai sauce

1 cup water

4 ounces rice noodles

½ cup bean sprouts

¼ cup unsalted peanuts, chopped

Optional toppings: sliced scallions, chopped fresh cilantro, lime wedges

1. Set the Instant Pot to Sauté and pour in 1 tablespoon of olive oil.

2. Once the oil is shimmering, add the egg and scramble until set. Press Cancel to turn off the Instant Pot and transfer the egg to a plate.

3. Add the remaining 1 tablespoon of olive oil, followed by the pad thai sauce, water, and rice noodles, leaving the noodles floating slightly above the other ingredients.

4. Lock the lid in place. Select Pressure Cook and adjust the pressure to High and the time to 2 minutes. After cooking, move the steam release handle to venting and quick release the pressure.

5. Once the float valve drops, open the lid and stir in the bean sprouts. Put the lid back on and let stand for 3 minutes.

6. Open the lid, add the egg, and stir. Sprinkle with the peanuts and serve warm with your favorite toppings.

VARIATION TIP: Add some shrimp to your pad thai! Simply cook in oil on Sauté and set aside while you cook the noodles, then add at the end with the egg.

Per Serving: Calories: 574; Carbohydrates: 59g; Fat: 31g; Fiber: 4g; Protein: 15g; Sugar: 7g; Sodium: 624mg

VEGETABLE LASAGNA

Serves 2

PREP & FINISHING: 5 minutes   **PRESSURE COOK:** 10 minutes on High
PRESSURE RELEASE: Quick   **TOTAL TIME:** 20 minutes

You're going to love how quick and easy this lasagna recipe comes together in your Instant Pot. No boiling noodles or fancy layering required—simply add your ingredients and cook for a delicious meal.

½ cup water

6 lasagna noodles, broken into 2-inch pieces

1 cup baby spinach, chopped

1 cup chunky vegetable pasta sauce

½ teaspoon salt

½ teaspoon black pepper

½ cup ricotta cheese

½ cup shredded mozzarella cheese

1. Pour the water into the Instant Pot.

2. Add the lasagna noodle pieces and spinach, then top with the pasta sauce and season with the salt and pepper.

3. Lock the lid in place. Select Pressure Cook and adjust the pressure to High and the time to 10 minutes. After cooking, move the steam release handle to venting and quick release the pressure.

4. Once the float valve drops, open the lid, add the ricotta, and stir.

5. Top the noodles with the mozzarella cheese, but do not stir. Put the lid back on the Instant Pot and let stand until the cheese is melted, about 3 minutes. Serve warm.

VARIATION TIP: Switch up your veggies! Try sliced mushrooms or zucchini.

Per Serving: Calories: 432; Carbohydrates: 51g; Fat: 15g; Fiber: 4g; Protein: 22g; Sugar: 6g; Sodium: 1,393mg

Meatless Mains

VEGGIE BURRITOS

Serves 2

PREP & FINISHING: 5 minutes   **PRESSURE COOK:** 4 minutes on High
PRESSURE RELEASE: Natural for 10 minutes, then Quick   **TOTAL TIME:** 24 minutes

These veggie burritos come together easily and are packed full of flavor. Feel free to customize the recipe with your favorite seasonal produce.

¾ cup white rice

1 (15-ounce) can black beans, rinsed and drained

1 cup frozen corn kernels

1 cup water

½ cup salsa (store-bought or homemade, page 119)

2 (10-inch) flour tortillas

Optional toppings: shredded cheddar cheese, diced avocado, chopped fresh cilantro

1. Combine the rice, beans, corn, and water in the Instant Pot and stir.

2. Top with the salsa, but do not stir.

3. Lock the lid in place. Select Pressure Cook and adjust the pressure to High and the time to 4 minutes. After cooking, let the pressure release naturally for 10 minutes, then quick release any remaining pressure.

4. Once the float valve drops, open the lid and stir to mix.

5. Spoon the filling into each tortilla and add any desired toppings, Roll up the burritos and serve warm.

VARIATION TIP: Instead of corn—or in addition to it—you can use any frozen veggies you like for a different flavor profile.

Per Serving: Calories: 744; Carbohydrates: 149g; Fat: 6g; Fiber: 18g; Protein: 25g; Sugar: 5g; Sodium: 975mg

VEGETABLE FRIED RICE

Serves 2

PREP & FINISHING: 5 minutes   **PRESSURE COOK:** 4 minutes on High
PRESSURE RELEASE: Natural for 10 minutes, then Quick   **SAUTÉ:** 6 minutes
TOTAL TIME: 30 minutes

Once you see how easily fried rice is made in the Instant Pot, you'll be hooked.

1 cup white rice

1 cup water

1 tablespoon sesame oil

2 teaspoons minced garlic

1 cup frozen peas and carrots

2 large eggs, lightly beaten

2 tablespoons soy sauce

Salt

Black pepper

Sliced scallions, for serving (optional)

1. Combine the rice and water in the Instant Pot and stir.

2. Lock the lid in place. Select Pressure Cook and adjust the pressure to High and the time to 4 minutes. After cooking, let the pressure release naturally for 10 minutes, then quick release any remaining pressure. Press Cancel to turn off the Instant Pot.

3. Fluff the rice with a fork, transfer to a bowl, and cover loosely to keep warm. Wipe out the inner pot.

4. Set the Instant Pot to Sauté and add the sesame oil.

5. Once the oil is shimmering, add the garlic and peas and carrots and cook, stirring occasionally, for 3 minutes.

6. Push the ingredients to the sides of the pot and add the eggs in the center. Cook, stirring constantly, until the eggs begin to set, then stir into the vegetable mixture until cooked through.

7. Press Cancel to turn off the Instant Pot, then fold in the cooked rice and soy sauce. Season with salt and pepper to taste. Top with sliced scallions (if using) and serve warm.

USE IT UP: Warm any leftovers and serve with Teriyaki Chicken (page 72).

Per Serving: Calories: 532; Carbohydrates: 87g; Fat: 12g; Fiber: 4g; Protein: 16g; Sugar: 0g; Sodium: 907mg

Meatless Mains

SPINACH PARMESAN PASTA

Serves 2

PREP & FINISHING: 10 minutes   **SAUTÉ:** 2 minutes   **PRESSURE COOK:** 8 minutes on High
PRESSURE RELEASE: Quick   **TOTAL TIME:** 25 minutes

A pasta dish for two that you can make in the Instant Pot? Sign me up! I love the combination of spinach in a Parmesan butter sauce—simple and delicious.

1 tablespoon olive oil

2 teaspoons minced garlic

4 ounces spaghetti, broken in half

1½ cups water

2 tablespoons butter

3 cups baby spinach

¼ cup grated Parmesan cheese

Salt

Black pepper

1. Set the Instant Pot to Sauté and pour in the olive oil.

2. Once the oil is shimmering, add the garlic and sauté for 1 minute. Press Cancel to turn off the Instant Pot.

3. Add the spaghetti and water and stir to separate spaghetti strands.

4. Lock the lid in place. Select Pressure Cook and adjust the pressure to High and the time to 8 minutes. After cooking, move the steam release handle to venting and quick release the pressure.

5. Once the float valve drops, open the lid and stir. Add the butter, spinach, and Parmesan cheese. Gently toss and cook until the spinach leaves are wilted. Season with salt and pepper to taste. Serve warm.

VARIATION TIP: Mushrooms go great in this dish. If you have leftover mushrooms from the Mushroom Risotto (page 54), slice them up and toss in for another delicious flavor option.

Per Serving: Calories: 439; Carbohydrates: 46g; Fat: 23g; Fiber: 3g; Protein: 12g; Sugar: 2g; Sodium: 356mg

SPAGHETTI SQUASH AND SAUCE

Serves 2

PREP & FINISHING: 5 minutes   **SAUTÉ:** 5 minutes   **PRESSURE COOK:** 10 minutes on High
PRESSURE RELEASE: Quick   **SIMMER:** 5 minutes   **TOTAL TIME:** 30 minutes

It's spaghetti without all the carbs! Cook up spaghetti squash and marinara sauce all in one go with this easy Instant Pot dish.

1 (2-pound) spaghetti squash

1 tablespoon olive oil

½ cup chopped onion

2 teaspoons minced garlic

¼ teaspoon dried oregano

¼ teaspoon salt, plus more to taste

⅛ teaspoon black pepper, plus more to taste

¼ cup water

1 (14.5-ounce) can diced tomatoes

Chopped fresh basil, for topping (optional)

1. With a fork or knife, carefully pierce the spaghetti squash skin multiple times and set aside.

2. Set the Instant Pot to Sauté and pour in the olive oil.

3. Once the oil is shimmering, add the onion and cook, stirring often, until the translucent, 3 to 4 minutes.

4. Add the garlic, oregano, salt, and pepper and sauté for another minute. Press Cancel to turn off the Instant Pot.

5. Pour in the water and scrape up any brown bits from the bottom of the pot.

6. Pour the tomatoes and juices over the onion, but do not stir.

7. Place a trivet over the tomatoes. Set the spaghetti squash on top of the trivet.

8. Lock the lid in place. Select Pressure Cook and adjust the pressure to High and the time to 10 minutes. After cooking, move the steam release handle to venting and quick release the pressure.

continued

Meatless Mains

9. Once the float valve drops, open the lid and carefully remove the spaghetti squash and trivet.

10. Set the Instant Pot to Sauté to simmer and cook for 5 minutes to thicken the sauce.

11. Cut the spaghetti squash in half lengthwise. Scoop out the seeds from the center and discard. Use a fork to scrape the strands of squash into a bowl.

12. Season the squash with salt and pepper to taste and top with the sauce. Garnish with fresh basil, if desired.

VARIATION TIP: Already have a favorite sauce on hand? Place a trivet in the bottom of the Instant Pot, then pour in 1 cup water. Set the spaghetti squash on top of the trivet and cook as directed above. Then just heat up your sauce to top the spaghetti squash.

Per Serving: Calories: 254; Carbohydrates: 43g; Fat: 10g; Fiber: 12g; Protein: 5g; Sugar: 19g; Sodium: 606mg

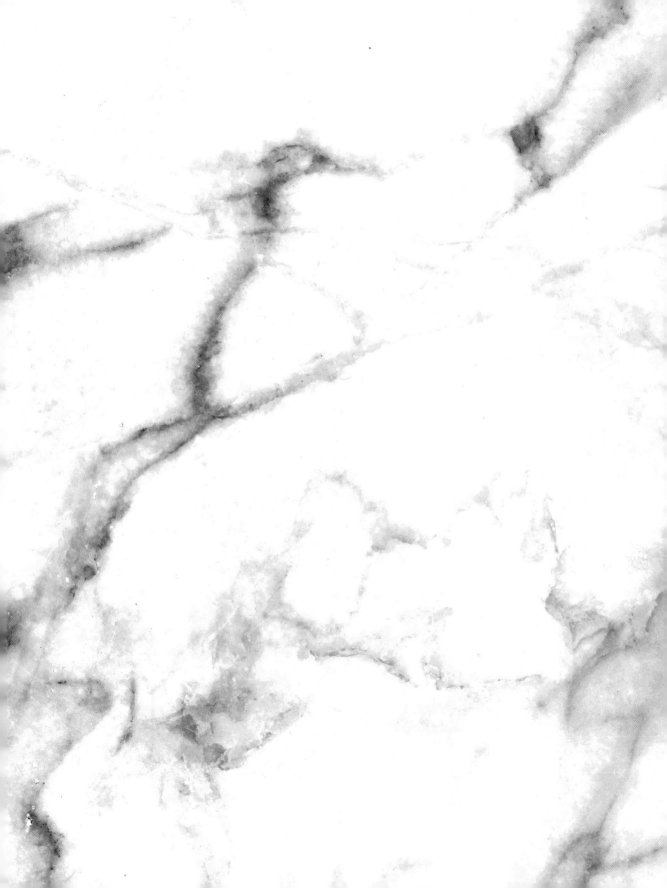

CHAPTER

CHICKEN AND SEAFOOD

CHICKEN AND BROCCOLI STIR-FRY

Serves 2

PREP & FINISHING: 10 minutes   **PRESSURE COOK:** 4 minutes on High
PRESSURE RELEASE: Quick   **SAUTÉ:** 3 minutes   **TOTAL TIME:** 22 minutes

Get ready for the easiest stir-fry you'll ever make. I love how quickly this meal comes together—just 30 minutes and dinner is on the table.

2 (5- to 6-ounce) bone-less, skinless chicken breasts, cut into 1-inch pieces

1 tablespoon packed light brown sugar

¼ cup soy sauce

1 teaspoon sesame oil

1 cup water, divided

1 tablespoon cornstarch

1 cup frozen broccoli florets

Sesame seeds, for garnish (optional)

1. Combine the chicken, brown sugar, soy sauce, sesame oil, and ¾ cup of water in the Instant Pot and stir.

2. Lock the lid in place. Select Pressure Cook and adjust the pressure to High and the time to 4 minutes. After cooking, move the steam release handle to venting and quick release the pressure.

3. Once the float valve drops, open the lid. Press Cancel to turn off the Instant Pot, then set the Instant Pot to Sauté.

4. In a small bowl, whisk together the cornstarch and remaining ¼ cup of water until completely dissolved. Pour the cornstarch slurry into the Instant Pot while whisk-ing the sauce.

5. Add the broccoli and stir until the broccoli cooks through and the sauce thickens, 2 to 3 minutes. Press Cancel to turn off the Instant Pot.

6. Serve warm, garnished with sesame seeds if you like.

VARIATION TIP: Feel free to add more veggies. The sauce in this dish pairs well with a variety of vegetables, such as carrots, onions, and mushrooms.

Per Serving: Calories: 191; Carbohydrates: 16g; Fat: 4g; Fiber: 3g; Protein: 24g; Sugar: 8g; Sodium: 1,517mg

CHICKEN TACOS

Serves 2

PREP & FINISHING: 5 minutes   **PRESSURE COOK:** 15 minutes on High
PRESSURE RELEASE: Natural for 5 minutes, then Quick   **TOTAL TIME:** 30 minutes

It can be Taco Tuesday any day of the week with these delicious and easy chicken tacos. Whip up some salsa chicken in your Instant Pot and serve with tortillas and your choice of toppings for a meal that is truly your own.

½ cup salsa (store-bought or homemade, page 119)

½ cup chicken broth (store-bought or home-made, page 116)

1 tablespoon olive oil

½ teaspoon salt

2 (5- to 6-ounce) boneless, skinless chicken breasts

4 (8-inch) corn tortillas

Optional toppings: shredded cheddar cheese, sliced onion, sliced avocado, chopped fresh cilantro

1. Combine the salsa, broth, olive oil, and salt in the Instant Pot.

2. Nestle the chicken breasts into the salsa mixture.

3. Lock the lid in place. Select Pressure Cook and adjust the pressure to High and the time to 15 minutes. After cooking, let the pressure release naturally for 5 minutes, then quick release any remaining pressure.

4. Once the float valve drops, open the lid and transfer the chicken to a plate or cutting board.

5. Shred the chicken with two forks, then return the meat to the salsa mixture and stir it in.

6. Serve the chicken warm on corn tortillas with your favorite toppings.

USE IT UP: Have leftover chicken? Add it to a tortilla with cheese for an easy chicken quesadilla.

Per Serving: Calories: 316; Carbohydrates: 35g; Fat: 10g; Fiber: 5g; Protein: 23g; Sugar: 3g; Sodium: 890mg

Chicken and Seafood

TERIYAKI CHICKEN

Serves 2

PREP & FINISHING: 10 minutes   **SAUTÉ:** 7 minutes   **PRESSURE COOK:** 8 minutes on High
PRESSURE RELEASE: Natural for 5 minutes, then Quick   **TOTAL TIME:** 35 minutes

This is one of my favorite ways to prepare chicken. The teriyaki sauce is simple but healthier and better tasting than anything you'll find in a bottle at the grocery store. Serve over steamed rice.

1 tablespoon sesame oil

3 (4- to 5-ounce) boneless, skinless chicken thighs

¼ teaspoon salt

⅛ teaspoon black pepper

½ cup water, divided

2 teaspoons minced garlic

¼ cup soy sauce

¼ cup packed light brown sugar

1 tablespoon cornstarch

1. Set the Instant Pot to Sauté and pour in the sesame oil.

2. Season the chicken thighs with the salt and pepper. Once the oil is shimmering, put the thighs into the Instant Pot and allow them to sear for 2 minutes on each side. Press Cancel to turn off the Instant Pot. Transfer the thighs to a plate.

3. Pour ¼ cup of water into the Instant Pot and scrape up any brown bits from the bottom of the pot.

4. Add the garlic, soy sauce, and brown sugar and stir. Return the chicken thighs to the pot and stir to coat.

5. Lock the lid in place. Select Pressure Cook and adjust the pressure to High and the time to 8 minutes. After cooking, let the pressure release naturally for 5 minutes, then quick release any remaining pressure.

6. Once the float valve drops, open the lid. Press Cancel to turn off the Instant Pot, then set the Instant Pot to Sauté. Transfer the chicken thighs to a clean plate.

7. In a small bowl, whisk together the cornstarch and remaining ¼ cup of water until completely dissolved. Pour the cornstarch slurry into the Instant Pot while whisking the sauce. Allow to cook for 2 to 3 minutes, stirring occasionally, until the sauce has thickened. Press Cancel to turn off the Instant Pot.

8. Serve the chicken thighs warm, topped with the thickened sauce.

SUBSTITUTION TIP: I prefer chicken thighs over breasts here for added flavor, but you can substitute boneless, skinless breasts in this recipe without any other modifications.

Per Serving: Calories: 458; Carbohydrates: 33g; Fat: 16g; Fiber: 0g; Protein: 44g; Sugar: 26g; Sodium: 2,254mg

CHICKEN MARSALA

Serves 2

PREP & FINISHING: 10 minutes **SAUTÉ:** 10 minutes **PRESSURE COOK:** 8 minutes on High
PRESSURE RELEASE: Natural for 5 minutes, then Quick **TOTAL TIME:** 38 minutes

In this simple marsala recipe, panfried chicken breasts are cooked in sweet marsala wine with plenty of mushrooms and made perfectly decadent and creamy with a splash of heavy cream. Serve with crusty bread for getting every last drop of sauce.

1 tablespoon olive oil

¼ cup all-purpose flour, divided

2 (5- to 6-ounce) boneless, skinless chicken breasts

¼ teaspoon salt

⅛ teaspoon black pepper

½ cup water, plus 2 tablespoons, divided

1 cup sliced mushrooms

½ cup marsala wine

2 tablespoons heavy cream

1. Set the Instant Pot to Sauté and pour in the olive oil.

2. Set aside 1 tablespoon of flour for use later. Put the rest of the flour in a shallow dish. Season the chicken breasts with the salt and pepper, then dredge them in the flour. Once the oil is shimmering, add the chicken and cook until golden brown, 3 to 4 minutes per side. Press Cancel to turn off the Instant Pot and transfer the chicken to a plate.

3. Pour the water into the Instant Pot and scrape up any bits from the bottom of the pot.

4. Return the chicken to the pot and top with the mushrooms and wine.

5. Lock the lid in place. Select Pressure Cook and adjust the pressure to High and the time to 8 minutes. After cooking, let the pressure release naturally for 5 minutes, then quick release any remaining pressure.

6. Once the float valve drops, open the lid. Press Cancel to turn off the Instant Pot, then set the Instant Pot to Sauté. Transfer the chicken breasts to a clean plate.

7. In a small bowl, whisk together the reserved 1 tablespoon of flour and the remaining 2 tablespoons of water until completely dissolved. Pour the flour slurry into the Instant Pot while whisking the sauce.

8. Allow to cook for 2 to 3 minutes, stirring occasionally, until the sauce has thickened. Stir in the heavy cream. Press Cancel to turn off the Instant Pot.

9. Serve the chicken breasts warm, topped with the mushroom sauce.

VARIATION TIP: Add crumbled Gorgonzola cheese along with the cream for a rich, earthy flavor.

Per Serving: Calories: 456; Carbohydrates: 22g; Fat: 15g; Fiber: 1g; Protein: 40g; Sugar: 6g; Sodium: 391mg

CHICKEN AND MARINARA SAUCE

Serves 2

PREP & FINISHING: 10 minutes   **SAUTÉ:** 10 minutes   **PRESSURE COOK:** 8 minutes on High
PRESSURE RELEASE: Natural for 5 minutes, then Quick   **TOTAL TIME:** 38 minutes

Break out the wine, it's Italian night! This is a delicious way to serve chicken, topped with your favorite marinara sauce and plenty of melty mozzarella cheese. Pair with your favorite pasta for a dish everyone will love.

1 tablespoon olive oil

2 (5- to 6-ounce) boneless, skinless chicken breasts

2 teaspoons Italian seasoning

¼ teaspoon salt

⅛ teaspoon black pepper

½ cup water

1 cup marinara sauce

1 cup shredded mozzarella cheese

1. Set the Instant Pot to Sauté and pour in the olive oil.

2. Season the chicken breasts with the Italian seasoning, salt, and pepper. Once the oil is shimmering, add the chicken and cook until golden brown, 3 to 4 minutes per side. Press Cancel to turn off the Instant Pot and transfer the chicken to a plate.

3. Pour the water into the Instant Pot and scrape up any bits from the bottom of the pot.

4. Return the chicken breasts to the pot and top with the marinara sauce.

5. Lock the lid in place. Select Pressure Cook and adjust the pressure to High and the time to 8 minutes. After cooking, let the pressure release naturally for 5 minutes, then quick release any remaining pressure.

6. Once the float valve drops, open the lid. Scatter the cheese over the top, put the lid back on, and let stand until the cheese is melted, 2 to 3 minutes. Serve warm.

VARIATION TIP: This recipe also works with breaded chicken. Sub in breaded chicken fillets (or dredge the chicken breasts in flour and seasoning) and panfry before cooking with the marinara sauce.

Per Serving: Calories: 442; Carbohydrates: 8g; Fat: 22g; Fiber: 2g; Protein: 51g; Sugar: 5g; Sodium: 1,107mg

CHICKEN ALFREDO

Serves 2

PREP & FINISHING: 10 minutes   **SAUTÉ:** 7 minutes   **PRESSURE COOK:** 6 minutes on High
PRESSURE RELEASE: Quick   **TOTAL TIME:** 30 minutes

Creamy chicken Alfredo is an Italian food lover's dream come true. Once you learn to make it in the Instant Pot, you can have it anytime cravings strike.

1 tablespoon olive oil

1 (5- to 6-ounce) boneless, skinless chicken breast, cut into 1-inch pieces

¼ teaspoon salt

¼ teaspoon black pepper

1 cup chicken broth (store-bought or homemade, page 116)

1 cup heavy cream

4 ounces fettuccine noodles, broken in half

1 cup grated Parmesan cheese

1. Set the Instant Pot to Sauté and pour in the olive oil.

2. Season the chicken with the salt and pepper. Once the oil is shimmering, add the chicken and cook until golden brown, 3 to 4 minutes. Press Cancel to turn off the Instant Pot and transfer the chicken to a plate.

3. Add the broth to the Instant Pot and scrape up any bits from the bottom of the pot.

4. Add the heavy cream and fettuccine to the Instant Pot and stir, then top with the chicken.

5. Lock the lid in place. Select Pressure Cook and adjust the pressure to High and the time to 6 minutes. After cooking, move the steam release handle to venting and quick release the pressure.

6. Once the float valve drops, open the lid. Stir the pasta and chicken, and slowly add the Parmesan cheese until melted. Serve warm.

VARIATION TIP: Try this recipe with blackened chicken. Season the chicken with cayenne pepper and garlic powder before browning in the Instant Pot for added flavor and a little kick.

Per Serving: Calories: 1,076; Carbohydrates: 52g; Fat: 68g; Fiber: 2g; Protein: 61g; Sugar: 5g; Sodium: 1,038mg

Chicken and Seafood

BURRITO BOWLS WITH CHICKEN AND BLACK BEANS

Serves 2

PREP & FINISHING: 10 minutes **PRESSURE COOK:** 10 minutes on High
PRESSURE RELEASE: Quick **TOTAL TIME:** 25 minutes

This easy one-pot meal is fully customizable. Starting with chicken, beans, rice, and a little bit of spice, there's no limit to the toppings you can add to make this dish your own.

1 (5- to 6-ounce) boneless, skinless chicken breast, cut into 1-inch pieces

1 tablespoon taco seasoning

½ cup long-grain rice

½ cup canned black beans, drained and rinsed

1 cup water

¾ cup salsa (store-bought or homemade, page 119)

Optional toppings: shredded cheddar cheese, sliced tomatoes, chopped fresh cilantro

1. Combine the chicken, taco seasoning, rice, beans, and water to the Instant Pot and stir.

2. Top with the salsa, but do not stir.

3. Lock the lid in place. Select Pressure Cook and adjust the pressure to High and the time to 10 minutes. After cooking, move the steam release handle to venting and quick release the pressure.

4. Once the float valve drops, open the lid. Stir the mixture. If using shredded cheese, add it now and put the lid back on until the cheese is melted, 2 to 3 minutes.

5. Serve warm, with cheese, tomatoes and cilantro, if using.

VARIATION TIP: Switch up the protein. This recipe calls for chicken but would also be delicious with Barbacoa (page 89) or Carnitas (page 97).

Per Serving: Calories: 446; Carbohydrates: 55g; Fat: 3g; Fiber: 6g; Protein: 46g; Sugar: 4g; Sodium: 775mg

BUFFALO WINGS

Serves 2

PREP & FINISHING: 5 minutes   **PRESSURE COOK:** 10 minutes on High
PRESSURE RELEASE: Quick   **SAUTÉ:** 5 minutes   **TOTAL TIME:** 20 minutes

Whether it's game day or just a lazy weekend, it's always good to have a reliable recipe for killer chicken wings. I love the richness that butter brings to the Buffalo sauce and how the Instant Pot cooks the wings up so tender!

2 pounds chicken wings (10 to 12 wings)

1 teaspoon garlic powder

¼ teaspoon salt

¼ teaspoon black pepper

4 tablespoons butter

½ cup Buffalo sauce

1. Place a trivet in the bottom of the Instant Pot, then pour in ¾ cup water.

2. Season the wings with the garlic powder, salt, and pepper, and place on top of the trivet.

3. Lock the lid in place. Select Pressure Cook and adjust the pressure to High and the time to 10 minutes. After cooking, move the steam release handle to venting and quick release the pressure.

4. Once the float valve drops, open the lid and carefully transfer the wings to a plate. Press Cancel to turn off the Instant Pot and wipe out the inner pot.

5. Set the Instant Pot to Sauté and add butter to the inner pot. Once melted, whisk in the hot sauce.

6. Return the wings to the pot and toss until coated with sauce. Serve warm.

VARIATION TIP: Like your wings a little crispy? Once they're out of the Instant Pot, spread them out on a baking sheet and cook under the broiler for a few minutes to caramelize the sauce.

Per Serving: Calories: 1,208; Carbohydrates: 2g; Fat: 95g; Fiber: 1g; Protein: 81g; Sugar: 0g; Sodium: 1,120mg

Chicken and Seafood

SHRIMP BOIL WITH BABY POTATOES AND CORN

Serves 2

PREP & FINISHING: 15 minutes   **PRESSURE COOK:** 6 minutes on High
PRESSURE RELEASE: Quick   **TOTAL TIME:** 26 minutes

Shrimp boils are a Southern favorite that features tender shrimp, hearty pota-toes, and sweet corn, all boiled together with Old Bay seasoning. They are usually made in big batches using a 12-quart stockpot, but here it's been conve-niently scaled down for just two people. Plus, the Instant Pot cuts conventional cooking time in half for a hearty meal that is on the table in no time.

8 ounces baby red potatoes

2 ears corn, husks and silk removed, cut in half

3 teaspoons Old Bay seasoning, divided

1 pound raw shrimp, peeled and deveined

⅓ cup butter, melted

Chopped fresh parsley, for garnish (optional)

Lemon, cut into wedges, for serving (optional)

1. Combine the potatoes and corn in the Instant Pot. Season with 2 teaspoons of Old Bay seasoning, then pour in ¾ cup water.

2. Lock the lid in place. Select Pressure Cook and adjust the pressure to High and the time to 5 minutes. After cooking, move the steam release handle to venting and quick release the pressure.

3. Once the float valve drops, open the lid. Add the shrimp.

4. Lock the lid in place again. Select Pressure Cook and adjust the pressure to High and the time to 1 minute. After cooking, move the steam release handle to venting and quick release the pressure.

5. Once the float valve drops, open the lid and drain the liquid from the inner pot. Season with the remaining 1 teaspoon of Old Bay and drizzle with the butter.

6. Garnish with parsley (if using) and serve warm with lemon wedges, if you like.

SUBSTITUTION TIP: Don't have Old Bay seasoning on hand? You can also use Cajun or Creole seasoning.

VARIATION TIP: If you like sliced andouille or other smoked sausage in your shrimp boil, add it with the potatoes and corn in step 1.

Per Serving: Calories: 698; Carbohydrates: 45g; Fat: 35g; Fiber: 6g; Protein: 53g; Sugar: 6g; Sodium: 1,956mg

SHRIMP SCAMPI

Serves 2

PREP & FINISHING: 10 minutes   **SAUTÉ:** 3 minutes   **PRESSURE COOK:** 3 minutes on High
PRESSURE RELEASE: Quick   **TOTAL TIME:** 21 minutes

In this simple but delicious dish, shrimp is sautéed in garlic and butter, which becomes the light and flavorful sauce for the angel-hair pasta. It comes together in less than 30 minutes for a satisfying and easy meal.

2 tablespoons butter

1 tablespoon olive oil

2 teaspoons minced garlic

1 pound raw shrimp, peeled and deveined

2 cups chicken broth (store-bought or home-made, page 116)

6 ounces angel-hair pasta, broken in half

Chopped fresh parsley, for garnish (optional)

Grated Parmesan cheese, for garnish (optional)

1. Set the Instant Pot to Sauté and put in the butter and olive oil.

2. Once the butter is melted and the oil is shimmering, add the garlic and shrimp and cook for 2 to 3 minutes, until fragrant. Press Cancel to turn off the Instant Pot.

3. Add the chicken broth and scrape up any bits from the bottom of the pot. Add the angel-hair pasta on top of the shrimp.

4. Lock the lid in place. Select Pressure Cook and adjust the pressure to High and the time to 3 minutes. After cooking, move the steam release handle to venting and quick release the pressure.

5. Once the float valve drops, stir the pasta and shrimp. Garnish with parsley and Parmesan cheese (if using) and serve warm.

VARIATION TIP: Add freshly squeezed lemon juice to the shrimp to add another layer of flavor to this delicious dish.

Per Serving: Calories: 674; Carbohydrates: 64g; Fat: 21g; Fiber: 3g; Protein: 57g; Sugar: 2g; Sodium: 367mg

OLD BAY CRAB LEGS

Serves 2

PREP & FINISHING: 10 minutes   **PRESSURE COOK:** 2 minutes on High
PRESSURE RELEASE: Quick   **TOTAL TIME:** 17 minutes

I love serving crab legs alongside a juicy steak for a special surf-and-turf dinner. This recipe takes advantage of a simple Old Bay and lemon seasoning to enhance the sweet and delicate flavor of the crab.

1 cup water

1 tablespoon Old Bay seasoning

1 lemon, sliced into rounds

2 pounds crab legs

1. Pour 1 cup water into the Instant Pot and stir in the Old Bay seasoning.

2. Place a trivet in the pot and layer the lemon slices on top. Arrange the crab legs on top of the lemon slices.

3. Lock the lid in place. Select Pressure Cook and adjust the pressure to High and the time to 2 minutes. After cooking, move the steam release handle to venting and quick release the pressure.

4. Once the float valve drops, open the lid. Carefully remove the crab legs and serve warm.

SUBSTITUTION TIP: Don't have Old Bay seasoning on hand? You can also use Cajun or Creole seasoning.

Per Serving: Calories: 300; Carbohydrates: 1g; Fat: 4g; Fiber: 0g; Protein: 61g; Sugar: 1g; Sodium: 2,755mg

Chicken and Seafood

LEMON-PEPPER SALMON

Serves 2

PREP & FINISHING: 10 minutes   **PRESSURE COOK:** 3 minutes on Low

PRESSURE RELEASE: Quick   **TOTAL TIME:** 15 minutes

This lemon-pepper salmon comes together in just minutes with the help of the Instant Pot. It's a great recipe for those who are new to cooking fish at home—the result is a flaky and flavorful salmon.

1 pound salmon with skin	½ teaspoon lemon-pepper seasoning	2 dill sprigs
1 tablespoon butter, melted	¼ teaspoon salt	1 lemon, sliced into rounds

1. Place a trivet in the bottom of the Instant Pot, then pour in ¾ cup water.

2. Place the salmon on the trivet, skin-side down. Drizzle with the butter and season with lemon-pepper seasoning and salt. Place the dill sprigs on top, followed by the lemon slices.

3. Lock the lid in place. Select Pressure Cook and adjust the pressure to Low and the time to 3 minutes. After cooking, move the steam release handle to venting and quick release the pressure.

4. Once the float valve drops, open the lid. Carefully remove the salmon and serve warm.

SUBSTITUTION TIP: You can use any fresh herb you have on hand—such as rosemary, basil, or thyme—in place of the dill.

Per Serving: Calories: 373; Carbohydrates: 0g; Fat: 20g; Fiber: 0g; Protein: 45g; Sugar: 0g; Sodium: 436mg

CHAPTER

BEEF AND PORK

BARBECUE PULLED PORK

Serves 2

PREP & FINISHING: 10 minutes   **SAUTÉ:** 10 minutes   **PRESSURE COOK:** 1 hour on High
PRESSURE RELEASE: Natural for 20 minutes, then Quick   **TOTAL TIME:** 1 hour 45 minutes

You're going to love how easily this pulled pork comes together, and in a fraction of the conventional cooking time thanks to the Instant Pot. It's tender, juicy, and full of flavor.

1 tablespoon packed dark brown sugar

1 teaspoon garlic powder

1 teaspoon onion powder

½ teaspoon salt

½ teaspoon black pepper

1 (2-pound) boneless pork shoulder or pork butt, cut in half

1 tablespoon olive oil

¾ cup water

½ cup barbecue sauce

1. In a small bowl, mix the brown sugar, garlic powder, onion powder, salt, and pepper. Rub the seasoning all over the pork.

2. Set the Instant Pot to Sauté and pour in the olive oil. Once the oil is shimmering, add the pork to the Instant Pot and sear on each side for 2 minutes. Press Cancel to turn off the Instant Pot and transfer the pork to a plate.

3. Pour the water into the Instant Pot and scrape up any bits from the bottom of the pot. Return the pork to the pot.

4. Lock the lid in place. Select Pressure Cook and adjust the pressure to High and the time to 1 hour. After cooking, let the pressure release naturally for 20 minutes, then quick release any remaining pressure.

5. Once the float valve drops, open the lid. Carefully transfer the pork to a large bowl and shred with two forks. Add the barbecue sauce and stir to coat, then serve warm.

USE IT UP: Have leftover pulled pork? Pile it on a bun with some pickled red onions for a delicious pulled pork sandwich.

Per Serving: Calories: 1,064; Carbohydrates: 38g; Fat: 63g; Fiber: 1g; Protein: 80g; Sugar: 30g; Sodium: 1,596mg

BARBACOA

Serves: 2

PREP & FINISHING: 15 minutes **SAUTÉ:** 10 minutes **PRESSURE COOK:** 25 minutes on High
PRESSURE RELEASE: Natural for 5 minutes, then Quick **TOTAL TIME:** 1 hour

Barbacoa is one of my favorite things to order at a restaurant, so it's a recipe that I was determined to perfect for the Instant Pot. It's tender, juicy, and full of spice and flavor—great in tacos, burritos, and more!

1 tablespoon olive oil

1 pound chuck roast

Salt

Black pepper

1 cup beef broth, divided

2 teaspoons minced garlic

1 tablespoon apple cider vinegar

1 canned chipotle pepper in adobo sauce, plus 1 tablespoon adobo sauce

1 tablespoon lime juice (optional)

1. Set the Instant Pot to Sauté and pour in the olive oil.

2. Season the chuck roast all over with salt and pepper. Once the oil is shimmering, add the chuck roast and sear on each side for 4 to 5 minutes. Press Cancel to turn off the Instant Pot and transfer the roast to a plate.

3. Add ¼ cup of beef broth to the pot and scrape up any brown bits from the bottom of the pot.

4. Return the chuck roast to the pot and top with the garlic, vinegar, and chipotle pepper and adobo sauce. Pour the remaining ¾ cup of beef broth over the roast.

5. Lock the lid in place. Select Pressure Cook and adjust the pressure to High and the time to 25 minutes. After cooking, let the pressure release naturally for 5 minutes, then quick release any remaining pressure.

Beef and Pork

continued

6. Once the float valve drops, open the lid. Using two forks, shred the beef into bite-size pieces inside the inner pot. Toss the beef with the juices, then cover and let the barbacoa beef soak up the juices for an extra 10 minutes. Stir in the lime juice (if using) and serve warm.

SUBSTITUTION TIP: You can also use brisket or a round roast for this recipe.
VARIATION TIP: Add additional chipotle peppers to add more heat to the juices.

Per Serving: Calories: 533; Carbohydrates: 3g; Fat: 38g; Fiber: 0g; Protein: 44g; Sugar: 1g; Sodium: 175mg

GARLIC-SOY SHORT RIBS

Serves 2

PREP & FINISHING: 10 minutes   **PRESSURE COOK:** 25 minutes on High
PRESSURE RELEASE: Quick   **SAUTÉ:** 5 minutes   **TOTAL TIME:** 45 minutes

The tender rib meat soaks up the flavor of the garlic-soy and brown sugar glaze.

¼ cup packed light brown sugar

1 tablespoon minced garlic

¼ cup soy sauce

1 tablespoon sesame oil

1½ pounds flanken-style short ribs, cut into 2-inch pieces

1 cup plus 1 table-spoon water

1 tablespoon cornstarch

Sliced scallions, for garnish (optional)

Sesame seeds, for garnish (optional)

1. In a small bowl, mix the brown sugar, garlic, soy sauce, and sesame oil.

2. Add the short ribs to the Instant Pot. Cover with the sauce mixture and pour in 1 cup of water.

3. Lock the lid in place. Select Pressure Cook and adjust the pressure to High and the time to 25 minutes. After cooking, move the steam release handle to venting and quick release the pressure.

4. Once the float valve drops, open the lid. Press Cancel to turn off the Instant Pot. Using a slotted spoon, transfer the short ribs to a serving dish.

5. In a small bowl, whisk together the cornstarch and remaining 1 tablespoon of water until completely dissolved. Pour the cornstarch slurry into the Instant Pot while whisking the sauce. Cook for 2 to 3 minutes, stirring occasionally, until the sauce has thickened to a glaze. Press Cancel to turn off the Instant Pot.

6. Pour the glaze over the short ribs and toss to coat. Serve warm, garnished with sliced scallions and sesame seeds, if desired.

VARIATION TIP: For crispy ribs, after step 4, spread them out on a baking sheet and cook under the broiler for a few minutes to caramelize the glaze.

Per Serving: Calories: 751; Carbohydrates: 33g; Fat: 37g; Fiber: 1g; Protein: 71g; Sugar: 27g; Sodium: 2,077mg

Beef and Pork

CLASSIC POT ROAST

Serves: 2

PREP & FINISHING: 10 minutes **SAUTÉ:** 10 minutes **PRESSURE COOK:** 25 minutes on High
PRESSURE RELEASE: Natural for 5 minutes, then Quick **TOTAL TIME:** 55 minutes

When it's time for a nourishing Sunday dinner, what's better than a tender pot roast served with hearty potatoes and flavorful carrots? This roast is easy to make and is done in less than an hour with the help of the Instant Pot.

1 tablespoon olive oil	½ teaspoon black pepper	6 small Yukon Gold or red potatoes
1 pound chuck roast	1 cup beef broth, divided	1 (2-ounce) package onion soup mix
½ teaspoon salt	1 cup baby carrots	

1. Set the Instant Pot to Sauté and pour in the olive oil.

2. Season the chuck roast all over with the salt and pepper. Once the oil is shimmering, add the chuck roast and sear on each side for 4 to 5 minutes. Press Cancel to turn off the Instant Pot and transfer the roast to a plate.

3. Add ¼ cup of beef broth to the Instant Pot and scrape up any browned bits from the bottom of the pot.

4. Return the roast to the pot, top with the carrots and potatoes, and sprinkle with the onion soup mix. Pour the remaining ¾ cup of beef broth over everything.

5. Lock the lid in place. Select Pressure Cook and adjust the pressure to High and the time to 25 minutes. After cooking, let the pressure release naturally for 5 minutes, then quick release any remaining pressure.

6. Once the float valve drops, open the lid and transfer the roast to a cutting board. Slice and serve warm with the carrots and potatoes.

SUBSTITUTION TIP: Bell peppers, onions, and mushrooms are great with a roast.

VARIATION TIP: You can also use a round roast or brisket for this recipe.

Per Serving: Calories: 905; Carbohydrates: 88g; Fat: 39g; Fiber: 11g; Protein: 53g; Sugar: 10g; Sodium: 987mg

SMALL-BATCH MEAT LOAF

Serves 2

PREP & FINISHING: 15 minutes   **PRESSURE COOK:** 45 minutes on High
PRESSURE RELEASE: Natural for 5 minutes, then Quick   **TOTAL TIME:** 55 minutes

Craving the nostalgic taste of Mom's meat loaf? This recipe is full of flavor and cooked just right, for a meat loaf for two that comes together with just a few ingredients and a little time.

8 ounces ground beef

1 large egg, beaten

¼ cup bread crumbs

⅓ cup finely chopped onion

¼ teaspoon salt

¼ teaspoon black pepper

¼ cup chili sauce

1. Place a trivet in the bottom of the Instant Pot, then pour in ½ cup water.

2. In a large bowl, combine the ground beef, egg, bread crumbs, onion, salt, and pepper. Mix well with your hands, then form the mixture into a small loaf.

3. Place the loaf in the center of a sheet of aluminum foil. Pull the corners and sides of the foil up, but do not seal. Place the foil and meat loaf on the trivet.

4. Lock the lid in place. Select Pressure Cook and adjust the pressure to High and the time to 45 minutes. After cooking, let the pressure release naturally for 5 minutes, then quick release any remaining pressure.

5. Once the float valve drops, open the lid and carefully lift out the foil with the meat loaf. Transfer the meat loaf to a serving plate and top with the chili sauce. Serve warm.

SUBSTITUTION TIP: Are you a fan of ketchup with meat loaf? You can easily substitute ketchup for the chili sauce in this recipe.

Per Serving: Calories: 335; Carbohydrates: 19g; Fat: 14g; Fiber: 3g; Protein: 29g; Sugar: 6g; Sodium: 958mg

Beef and Pork

TACO PASTA

Serves: 2

PREP & FINISHING: 5 minutes   **SAUTÉ:** 10 minutes   **PRESSURE COOK:** 5 minutes on High
PRESSURE RELEASE: Quick   **TOTAL TIME:** 25 minutes

All the flavors of Taco Tuesday come together in this easy one-pot pasta dish. The taco seasoning and salsa bring the heat, while the cheese balances out the dish and makes it rich and creamy.

8 ounces ground beef

¼ teaspoon salt

⅛ teaspoon
black pepper

1 tablespoon taco
seasoning

1 cup salsa (store-
bought or homemade,
page 119)

1 cup water

1 cup small shell pasta

1 cup shredded ched-
dar cheese

1. Set the Instant Pot to Sauté and add the ground beef. Season with the salt and pepper and cook, stirring often to break up the meat, until no longer pink. Press Cancel to turn off the Instant Pot.

2. Sprinkle the taco seasoning on top of the beef, then add the salsa and cover with the water. Do not stir. Add the pasta last, pushing it down into the liquid.

3. Lock the lid in place. Select Pressure Cook and adjust the pressure to High and the time to 5 minutes. After cooking, move the steam release handle to venting and quick release the pressure.

4. Once the float valve drops, open the lid and stir the pasta. Add the shredded cheese and stir until the cheese has melted. Serve warm.

SUBSTITUTION TIP: Don't have small shell pasta on hand? This taco pasta works well with any noodles you have, from rotini to macaroni.

Per Serving: Calories: 675; Carbohydrates: 51g; Fat: 31g; Fiber: 5g; Protein: 45g; Sugar: 7g; Sodium: 1,559mg

BARBECUE BABY BACK RIBS

Serves 2

PREP & FINISHING: 10 minutes   **PRESSURE COOK:** 20 minutes on High
PRESSURE RELEASE: Natural for 5 minutes, then Quick   **TOTAL TIME:** 40 minutes

No need to clean off the grill for this recipe, as the Instant Pot makes easy work of barbecue ribs. These ribs come out tender, juicy, and full of flavor. Serve with a side of Potato Salad (page 33) and you have yourself a full barbecue meal.

1 (1- to 1½-pound) rack baby back pork ribs, membrane removed

1 tablespoon barbecue seasoning

1 cup chicken broth (store-bought or homemade, page 116)

3 tablespoons apple cider vinegar

½ cup barbecue sauce

1. Season the ribs on both sides with the seasoning.

2. Place a trivet in the bottom of the Instant Pot, then pour in the chicken broth and vinegar.

3. Stand the rack of ribs on top of the trivet, wrapping the rack around the inside of the inner pot.

4. Lock the lid in place. Select Pressure Cook and adjust the pressure to High and the time to 20 minutes. After cooking, let the pressure release naturally for 5 minutes, then quick release any remaining pressure.

5. Once the float valve drops, open the lid and transfer the ribs to a serving plate. Brush with the barbecue sauce and serve warm.

VARIATION TIP: Like your ribs a little crispy? Once they're out of the Instant Pot, place the ribs on a baking sheet and put it under the broiler for a few minutes to caramelize the sauce.

Per Serving: Calories: 459; Carbohydrates: 32g; Fat: 13g; Fiber: 1g; Protein: 48g; Sugar: 24g; Sodium: 1,197mg

PORK CHOPS AND GRAVY

Serves 2

PREP & FINISHING: 10 minutes   **SAUTÉ:** 3 minutes   **PRESSURE COOK:** 5 minutes on High
PRESSURE RELEASE: Natural for 10 minutes, then Quick   **TOTAL TIME:** 33 minutes

The Instant Pot will give you pork chops that are tender and juicy on the inside.

1 tablespoon packed light brown sugar

1 teaspoon salt, divided

1 teaspoon black pepper, divided

2 (5- to 6-ounce) bone-less pork chops

1 tablespoon butter

1 cup chicken broth (store-bought or home-made, page 116)

1 tablespoon cornstarch

1 tablespoon water

1. In a small bowl, mix the brown sugar, ½ teaspoon of salt, and ½ teaspoon of pepper. Season the pork chops on both sides with the mixture.

2. Set the Instant Pot to Sauté and put in the butter. Once the pot is hot and the butter is melted, add the pork chops and brown for 1 to 2 minutes per side. Press Cancel to turn off the Instant Pot and transfer the pork chops to a plate.

3. Pour the broth into the Instant Pot and scrape up any brown bits from the bottom of the pot. Return the pork chops to the pot.

4. Lock the lid in place. Select Pressure Cook and adjust the pressure to High and the time to 5 minutes. After cooking, let the pressure release naturally for 10 minutes, then quick release any remaining pressure.

5. Once the float valve drops, open the lid. Carefully remove the pork chops and set aside.

6. In a small bowl, whisk together the cornstarch and water. Set the Instant Pot to Sauté. Pour the cornstarch slurry into the pot while whisking the gravy. Cook for 2 to 3 minutes, stirring occasionally, until the gravy has thickened. Press Cancel to turn off the Instant Pot.

7. Serve the pork chops warm, with the gravy.

VARIATION TIP: Replace the brown sugar with garlic and sliced mushrooms.

Per Serving: Calories: 356; Carbohydrates: 10g; Fat: 17g; Fiber: 0g; Protein: 37g; Sugar: 7g; Sodium: 1,292mg

CARNITAS

Serves 2

PREP & FINISHING: 10 minutes   **SAUTÉ:** 15 minutes
PRESSURE COOK: 30 minutes on High   **PRESSURE RELEASE:** Natural for
15 minutes, then Quick   **TOTAL TIME:** 1 hour 15 minutes

Carnitas, or Mexican pulled pork, is the perfect filling for tacos or burritos.

1 tablespoon olive oil

1 pound boneless
pork roast

¼ teaspoon salt

¼ teaspoon
black pepper

¾ cup chicken broth
(store-bought or home-
made, page 116)

2 tablespoons taco
seasoning

¼ cup orange juice

1 tablespoon lime juice

1. Set the Instant Pot to Sauté and pour in the olive oil.

2. Season the pork roast with the salt and pepper. Once the oil is shimmering, add the pork and allow it to sear on each side for 2 to 3 minutes. Transfer the pork to a plate.

3. Press Cancel to turn off the Instant Pot. Add ¼ cup of broth to the pot and scrape up any brown bits from the bottom. Return the pork to the pot.

4. In a small bowl, combine the taco seasoning, remaining ½ cup of broth, orange juice, and lime juice. Pour the mixture over the pork.

5. Lock the lid in place. Select Pressure Cook and adjust the pressure to High and the time to 30 minutes. After cooking, let the pressure release naturally for 15 minutes, then quick release any remaining pressure.

6. Once the float valve drops, open the lid. Press Cancel to turn off the Instant Pot. Using two forks, shred the pork into bite-size pieces inside the inner pot.

7. Set the Instant Pot to Sauté and cook the shredded pork until the liquid has reduced. Press Cancel to turn off the Instant Pot. Serve warm.

Per Serving: Calories: 481; Carbohydrates: 9g; Fat: 25g; Fiber: 1g; Protein: 49g; Sugar: 4g; Sodium: 814mg

Beef and Pork

PORK TENDERLOIN

Serves 2

PREP & FINISHING: 10 minutes   **SAUTÉ:** 15 minutes   **PRESSURE COOK:** 3 minutes on High

PRESSURE RELEASE: Natural for 10 minutes, then Quick   **TOTAL TIME:** 43 minutes

The Instant Pot is great for whipping up an easy pork tenderloin that is tender and full of flavor. Serve with Baked Potatoes (page 32) and Brussels Sprouts (page 30) for a complete meal.

2 tablespoons olive oil, divided

1 (8-ounce) pork tenderloin

2 teaspoons Italian seasoning

½ teaspoon salt

2 teaspoons minced garlic

½ cup chicken broth (store-bought or homemade, page 116)

1 tablespoon cornstarch

1 tablespoon water

1. Set the Instant Pot to Sauté and pour in 1 tablespoon of olive oil.

2. Season the tenderloin all over with the Italian seasoning and salt. Once the oil is shimmering, add the tenderloin and allow it to sear on each side for 4 to 5 minutes. Transfer the tenderloin to a plate.

3. Add the remaining 1 tablespoon of olive oil and the garlic to the Instant Pot. Sauté for 1 minute, or until the garlic is fragrant. Press Cancel to turn off the Instant Pot.

4. Add the broth to the pot and scrape up any bits from the bottom of the pot. Return the tenderloin to the pot.

5. Lock the lid in place. Select Pressure Cook and adjust the pressure to High and the time to 3 minutes. After cooking, let the pressure release naturally for 10 minutes, then quick release any remaining pressure.

6. Once the float valve drops, open the lid. Test the temperature of the pork to ensure it is at least 145°F. If needed, lock the lid back in place and allow the tenderloin to cook a little longer in the residual heat. Transfer the tenderloin to a cutting board.

7. In a small bowl, whisk together the cornstarch and water. Set the Instant Pot to Sauté. Pour the cornstarch slurry into the Instant Pot while whisking the sauce. Cook for 2 to 3 minutes, stirring occasionally, until the sauce has thickened. Press Cancel to turn off the Instant Pot.

8. Slice the tenderloin and serve warm with the sauce.

VARIATION TIP: Switch up the seasoning. Use your favorite pork rub instead of the Italian seasoning for your own take on this pork tenderloin recipe.

Per Serving: Calories: 277; Carbohydrates: 5g; Fat: 18g; Fiber: 1g; Protein: 24g; Sugar: 0g; Sodium: 642mg

PINEAPPLE-GLAZED HAM

Serves 2

PREP & FINISHING: 10 minutes   **PRESSURE COOK:** 15 minutes on High
PRESSURE RELEASE: Natural for 5 minutes, then Quick   **TOTAL TIME:** 35 minutes

One of my favorite dishes during the holidays is a good ham. This recipe features the same flavors of the holiday headliner—sweet ham with a pineapple-sugar glaze—but is easy enough to make any night of the week.

⅓ cup packed light brown sugar	⅛ teaspoon ground allspice	1 pound boneless ham
1 (8-ounce) can pineapple tidbits	1 cup chicken broth (store-bought or homemade, page 116)	

1. In a medium bowl, mix the brown sugar, pineapple tidbits with their juices, and allspice.

2. Place a trivet in the bottom of the Instant Pot, then pour in the chicken broth.

3. Place the ham, cut-side down, on the trivet. Pour the pineapple mixture over the ham.

4. Lock the lid in place. Select Pressure Cook and adjust the pressure to High and the time to 15 minutes. After cooking, let the pressure release naturally for 5 minutes, then quick release any remaining pressure.

5. Once the float valve drops, open the lid and transfer the ham to a cutting board. Slice and serve warm.

VARIATION TIP: If you like a little glaze with your ham, once it's done cooking, remove the ham and set the Instant Pot to Sauté. Let the juices reduce to a nice glaze you can serve with your slices of ham.

Per Serving: Calories: 526; Carbohydrates: 51g; Fat: 15g; Fiber: 1g; Protein: 45g; Sugar: 47g; Sodium: 2,021mg

HAM HOCK AND BEANS

Serves 2

PREP & FINISHING: 10 minutes   **PRESSURE COOK:** 40 minutes on High
PRESSURE RELEASE: Natural for 10 minutes, then Quick   **TOTAL TIME:** 1 hour 5 minutes

This recipe is inspired by my childhood. I loved a good bowl of ham hock and beans with a side of corn bread. My mother always kept it simple, so I did here as well, and the Instant Pot does a great job of cooking up these pinto beans—no soaking required.

1 cup dried pinto beans

1 ham hock

½ cup diced onion

2 teaspoons minced garlic

1 teaspoon salt

½ teaspoon black pepper

4 cups chicken broth (store-bought or homemade, page 116)

1. Combine the pinto beans, ham hock, onion, garlic, salt, and pepper in the Instant Pot. Cover with the broth.

2. Lock the lid in place. Select Pressure Cook and adjust the pressure to High and the time to 40 minutes. After cooking, let the pressure release naturally for 10 minutes, then quick release any remaining pressure.

3. Once the float valve drops, open the lid. Transfer the ham hock to a bowl. Discard the bones, skin, and cartilage. Shred the meat and return it to the pot. Serve the ham and beans warm.

VARIATION TIP: If you want to soak your beans overnight before cooking, you can reduce the pressure cook time from 40 minutes to 15 minutes and reduce the chicken broth from 4 cups to 3 cups.

Per Serving: Calories: 385; Carbohydrates: 65g; Fat: 4g; Fiber: 16g; Protein: 27g; Sugar: 4g; Sodium: 1,176mg

CHAPTER

DESSERTS

STRAWBERRY CRISP

Serves 2

PREP & FINISHING: 15 minutes   **PRESSURE COOK:** 10 minutes on High
PRESSURE RELEASE: Natural for 5 minutes, then Quick   **TOTAL TIME:** 35 minutes

---

With a rolled oat and brown sugar topping, this sweet treat puts strawberries on display, where they should be. Serve warm, topped with vanilla ice cream.

Nonstick cooking spray

1 cup strawberries, hulled and quartered

⅓ cup packed light brown sugar, divided

¼ cup all-purpose flour

¼ cup rolled oats

¼ teaspoon salt

3 tablespoons butter, melted

Vanilla ice cream, for serving (optional)

1. Place a trivet in the bottom of the Instant Pot, then pour in 1 cup water. Spray a 6- or 7-inch round pan (whatever fits best in your Instant Pot) with cooking spray.

2. In a small bowl, toss the strawberries with 2 tablespoons of brown sugar and let them sit for 5 minutes. Pour the strawberries into the prepared pan.

3. In a medium bowl, combine the flour, oats, remaining brown sugar, and salt. Add the melted butter and stir until the mixture is crumbly. Scatter the topping over the strawberries.

4. Cover the pan tightly with aluminum foil and place on top of the trivet.

5. Lock the lid in place. Select Pressure Cook and adjust the pressure to High and the time to 10 minutes. After cooking, let the pressure release naturally for 5 minutes, then quick release any remaining pressure.

6. Once the float valve drops, open the lid and carefully remove the pan. Serve warm, topped with vanilla ice cream, if you like.

VARIATION TIP: You can swap in any kind of berry for the strawberries in this recipe, or combine them for a mixed-berry crisp.

Per Serving: Calories: 434; Carbohydrates: 64g; Fat: 19g; Fiber: 4g; Protein: 5g; Sugar: 39g; Sodium: 439mg

CHEESECAKE

Serves 2

PREP & FINISHING: 10 minutes   **PRESSURE COOK:** 25 minutes on High
PRESSURE RELEASE: Natural for 10 minutes, then Quick
TOTAL TIME: 50 minutes, plus chilling time

Is cheesecake the perfect dessert? It just might be. But it's one that I didn't make much at home until I owned an Instant Pot. The easy prep and rich, creamy texture will win you over.

| Nonstick cooking spray | 3 tablespoons butter, melted | 1 (8-ounce) package cream cheese, softened |
| ¾ cup crushed graham crackers | ½ cup sugar, divided | 2 large eggs |

1. Place a trivet in the bottom of the Instant Pot, then pour in 1 cup water. Spray a 6-inch springform pan with cooking spray.

2. In a small bowl, combine the crushed graham crackers, butter, and 2 tablespoons of sugar. Press the mixture evenly into the bottom of the prepared pan.

3. In a medium bowl, beat together the cream cheese and remaining 6 tablespoons of sugar. Add the eggs, one at a time, and beat until well mixed. Pour the mixture over the graham cracker crust. Place the pan on top of the trivet.

4. Lock the lid in place. Select Pressure Cook and adjust the pressure to High and the time to 25 minutes. After cooking, press Cancel to turn off the Instant Pot and let the pressure release naturally for 10 minutes, then quick release any remaining pressure.

5. Once the float valve drops, open the lid and carefully remove the pan. Allow to cool, then refrigerate for at least 4 hours. Serve chilled.

VARIATION TIP: Try topping your cheesecake with classic cherry topping or even a drizzle of Dulce de Leche (page 126).

Per Serving: Calories: 942; Carbohydrates: 79g; Fat: 64g; Fiber: 1g; Protein: 15g; Sugar: 61g; Sodium: 767mg

Desserts

PEACH COBBLER

Serves 2

PREP & FINISHING: 10 minutes   **PRESSURE COOK:** 30 minutes on High
PRESSURE RELEASE: Natural for 15 minutes, then Quick   **TOTAL TIME:** 1 hour

Peach cobbler with vanilla ice cream is one of my family's favorite desserts. I have adapted this recipe from my sister-in-law's favorite way to cook up cobbler for a crowd. It's easy in the Instant Pot and just as delicious.

Nonstick cooking spray

1 (8.5-ounce) can sliced peaches, drained

½ cup baking mix

¼ cup milk

¼ cup sugar

3 tablespoons butter, cut into 6 pieces

Generous pinch ground cinnamon (optional)

Vanilla ice cream, for serving (optional)

1. Place a trivet in the bottom of the Instant Pot, then pour in 1 cup water. Spray a 6- or 7-inch round pan (whatever fits best in your Instant Pot) with cooking spray.

2. Spread out the peaches in the bottom of the pan.

3. In a medium bowl, combine the baking mix, milk, and sugar and pour the mixture over the peaches. Scatter the butter pieces on top. Sprinkle with the cinnamon, if using.

4. Cover the pan tightly with aluminum foil and place on top of the trivet.

5. Lock the lid in place. Select Pressure Cook and adjust the pressure to High and the time to 30 minutes. After cooking, let the pressure release naturally for 15 minutes, then quick release any remaining pressure.

6. Once the float valve drops, open the lid and carefully remove the pan. Serve warm, topped with vanilla ice cream, if desired.

VARIATION TIP: Replace the peaches with any fruit pie filling, like apple or cherry, for an equally delicious dish.

Per Serving: Calories: 430; Carbohydrates: 61g; Fat: 19g; Fiber: 3g; Protein: 5g; Sugar: 37g; Sodium: 151mg

CRÈME BRÛLÉE

Serves 2

PREP & FINISHING: 10 minutes   **PRESSURE COOK:** 10 minutes on High
PRESSURE RELEASE: Quick   **TOTAL TIME:** 25 minutes, plus chilling time

Ooh la la! Crème brûlée is my favorite dessert of all time, so developing a recipe to make it in the Instant Pot was at the top of my list. The result is a rich and creamy custard that you're going to love.

¼ cup sugar

2 large egg yolks

¾ cup heavy cream

1 teaspoon pure vanilla extract

1. Place a trivet in the bottom of the Instant Pot, then pour in 1 cup water.

2. In a medium bowl, combine the sugar and egg yolks. Add the cream and vanilla, and whisk until combined.

3. Pour the mixture into two 6-ounce ramekins. Cover the ramekins tightly with aluminum foil and place side by side on top of the trivet.

4. Lock the lid in place. Select Pressure Cook and adjust the pressure to High and the time to 10 minutes. After cooking, move the steam release handle to venting and quick release the pressure.

5. Once the float valve drops, open the lid and carefully remove the ramekins. Remove the foil and allow the custards to cool, then refrigerate for at least 4 hours. Serve chilled.

VARIATION TIP: For a caramelized top, sprinkle sugar on top of the chilled custard and use a culinary torch to turn the sugar into a crunchy, caramelized glaze. Alternatively, place the sugar-topped ramekins on a baking sheet and broil until the tops are golden brown and bubbling, 5 to 10 minutes.

Per Serving: Calories: 465; Carbohydrates: 28g; Fat: 37g; Fiber: 0g; Protein: 5g; Sugar: 28g; Sodium: 43mg

Desserts

CARAMEL POPCORN

Serves 2

PREP & FINISHING: 10 minutes   **SAUTÉ:** 10 minutes   **TOTAL TIME:** 20 minutes

This recipe is a nod to my friends who are obsessed with caramel popcorn. And who can blame them? It's a delicious treat! And this version of the salty, buttery, caramel snack is made in no time in the Instant Pot.

2 tablespoons coconut oil

⅓ cup popcorn kernels

1 teaspoon salt

4 tablespoons butter

½ cup packed light brown sugar

2 tablespoons heavy cream

1 teaspoon vanilla extract

1. Set the Instant Pot to Sauté and put in the coconut oil.

2. Once the pot is hot and the oil has melted, add a few popcorn kernels to test. If the kernels pop, it is hot enough to add remaining kernels; if not, wait another minute or two. Stir well to coat the kernels evenly with the oil, then cover with the lid.

3. Once the kernels start to pop, cook for 2 to 3 minutes, then press Cancel to turn off the Instant Pot. Keep the lid on until the popping stops.

4. Transfer the popped popcorn to a bowl, toss with the salt, and set aside.

5. Set the Instant Pot to Sauté again and put in the butter.

6. Once the pot is hot and the butter has melted, add the brown sugar and stir to combine, then add the cream and vanilla. Cook, stirring constantly, until the sugar has dissolved and the mixture is a caramel consistency, 4 to 5 minutes.

7. Press Cancel to turn off the Instant Pot. Return the popcorn to the pot. Toss gently until the popcorn is evenly coated with caramel.

8. Transfer the caramel popcorn to a parchment-lined baking sheet to cool, then serve.

VARIATION TIP: Try tossing in some peanuts at the end to add a salty crunch to this sweet treat.

Per Serving: Calories: 742; Carbohydrates: 86g; Fat: 44g; Fiber: 6g; Protein: 6g; Sugar: 54g; Sodium: 1,370mg

RICE PUDDING

Serves 2

PREP & FINISHING: 5 minutes   **PRESSURE COOK:** 20 minutes on High
PRESSURE RELEASE: Natural for 10 minutes, then Quick   **TOTAL TIME:** 40 minutes

This recipe creates an old-fashioned rice pudding that is creamy, with the perfect amount of texture and sweetness. And it is done in no time with the help of the Instant Pot.

½ cup white rice

1 cup milk

¾ cup water

½ teaspoon pure vanilla extract

½ teaspoon ground cinnamon

⅛ teaspoon salt

¼ cup sweetened condensed milk

1. Combine the rice, milk, water, vanilla, cinnamon, and salt in the Instant Pot and stir.

2. Lock the lid in place. Select Pressure Cook and adjust the pressure to High and the time to 20 minutes. After cooking, let the pressure release naturally for 10 minutes, then quick release any remaining pressure.

3. Once the float valve drops, open the lid. Stir the sweetened condensed milk into the rice pudding until combined. Serve warm.

VARIATION TIP: While I prefer my rice pudding without raisins, if you love them in yours, feel free to add them with the condensed milk at the end. You can also top your rice pudding with dried fruits, chopped nuts, or even some granola.

Per Serving: Calories: 377; Carbohydrates: 66g; Fat: 8g; Fiber: 1g; Protein: 10g; Sugar: 27g; Sodium: 257mg

Desserts

APPLE DUMP CAKE

Serves 2

PREP & FINISHING: 10 minutes   **PRESSURE COOK:** 25 minutes on High
PRESSURE RELEASE: Quick   **TOTAL TIME:** 40 minutes

Who doesn't love a good dump cake? Just add all your ingredients to a pan and bake. And now the Instant Pot makes this dessert even easier. Fruit, cake mix, and butter come together in one delicious treat.

Nonstick cooking spray	½ cup yellow cake mix
1 cup canned apple pie filling	3 tablespoons butter, cut into pieces

1. Place a trivet in the bottom of the Instant Pot, then pour in 1 cup water. Spray a 6- or 7-inch round pan (whatever fits best in your Instant Pot) with cooking spray.

2. Pour the apple pie filling into the prepared pan and top with the yellow cake mix. Scatter the butter pieces on top of the yellow cake mix and place the pan on top of the trivet.

3. Lock the lid in place. Select Pressure Cook and adjust the pressure to High and the time to 25 minutes. After cooking, move the steam release handle to venting and quick release the pressure.

4. Once the float valve drops, open the lid and carefully remove the pan. Serve warm.

VARIATION TIP: You can use any canned fruit or fruit pie filling for this recipe—try cherry, peach, or even pineapple.

Per Serving: Calories: 942; Carbohydrates: 160g; Fat: 33g; Fiber: 4g; Protein: 6g; Sugar: 31g; Sodium: 812mg

CINNAMON APPLES

Serves 2

PREP & FINISHING: 15 minutes   **PRESSURE COOK:** 5 minutes on High
PRESSURE RELEASE: Quick   **TOTAL TIME:** 25 minutes

Cinnamon apples are one of my holiday favorites. Thanks to the Instant Pot, it's easy to whip them up any day of the year as a delicious side or dessert topping. Once you make them this way, you'll never go back.

2 Honeycrisp apples, peeled, cored, and sliced ½ inch thick

1½ teaspoons lemon juice

½ cup packed dark brown sugar

1½ teaspoons ground cinnamon

½ cup water

1 tablespoon cornstarch

1. In a medium bowl, toss the apple slices with the lemon juice.

2. Transfer the apple slices to the Instant Pot and cover with the brown sugar and cinnamon. Toss to coat the apples.

3. In a small bowl, whisk together the water and cornstarch and add the mixture to the apple slices. Stir to combine.

4. Lock the lid in place. Select Pressure Cook and adjust the pressure to High and the time to 5 minutes. After cooking, move the steam release handle to venting and quick release the pressure.

5. Once the float valve drops, open the lid. Stir the apple slices gently and serve warm.

SUBSTITUTION TIP: Don't have time to peel and slice? Try using a bag of presliced apples (with the peel). They will still turn out delicious.

Per Serving: Calories: 334; Carbohydrates: 87g; Fat: 0g; Fiber: 4g; Protein: 0g; Sugar: 75g; Sodium: 16mg

Desserts

PUMPKIN PIE

Serves 2

PREP & FINISHING: 10 minutes   **PRESSURE COOK:** 45 minutes on High
PRESSURE RELEASE: Natural for 10 minutes, then Quick
TOTAL TIME: 1 hour, plus chilling time

I'm one of those people who likes to enjoy pumpkin-flavored desserts year-round. This small-batch pumpkin pie comes together easily with a buttery shortbread crust and sweet filling.

Nonstick cooking spray

½ cup crushed short-bread cookies

2 tablespoons butter, melted

1 cup canned pumpkin pie filling

2 tablespoons milk

1 large egg, beaten

1. Place a trivet in the bottom of the Instant Pot, then pour in 1 cup water. Spray a 6-inch springform pan with cooking spray.

2. In a small bowl, combine the crushed shortbread cookies and butter. Press the mixture evenly into the bottom of the prepared pan.

3. In a medium bowl, combine the pumpkin pie filling, milk, and egg. Pour the mixture on top of the cookie crust. Cover the springform pan tightly with aluminum foil. Place the pan on top of trivet.

4. Lock the lid in place. Select Pressure Cook and adjust the pressure to High and the time to 45 minutes. After cooking, let the pressure release naturally for 10 minutes, then quick release any remaining pressure.

5. Once the float valve drops, open the lid and carefully remove the pan. Remove the foil and allow to cool, then refrigerate for at least 4 hours. Serve chilled.

SUBSTITUTION TIP: This recipe calls for canned pumpkin pie filling. You can substitute 1 cup canned pumpkin purée plus 1 teaspoon pumpkin pie spice.

Per Serving: Calories: 470; Carbohydrates: 59g; Fat: 24g; Fiber: 12g; Protein: 7g; Sugar: 8g; Sodium: 539mg

CHOCOLATE-HAZELNUT SOUFFLÉ

Serves 2

PREP & FINISHING: 15 minutes   **PRESSURE COOK:** 9 minutes on High
PRESSURE RELEASE: Quick   **TOTAL TIME:** 29 minutes

Are you nuts over Nutella? I'm a big fan of the hazelnut spread, and it sure does make for a delicious and easy soufflé. These mini cakes are rich, chocolaty, and delicious.

1 large egg plus 1 large egg yolk

2 tablespoons sugar

⅓ cup chocolate-hazelnut spread (such as Nutella)

2 tablespoons all-purpose flour

Nonstick cooking spray

Confectioners' sugar, for serving

1. Place a trivet in the bottom of the Instant Pot, then pour in 1 cup water.

2. In a medium bowl, combine the egg, egg yolk, and sugar, and whisk until smooth. Add the chocolate-hazelnut spread and whisk until smooth. Add the flour and whisk until smooth.

3. Spray two 6-ounce ramekins with cooking spray. Divide the Nutella mixture evenly between the ramekins. Place the ramekins side by side on top of the trivet.

4. Lock the lid in place. Select Pressure Cook and adjust the pressure to High and the time to 9 minutes. After cooking, move the steam release handle to venting and quick release the pressure.

5. Once the float valve drops, open the lid and carefully remove the ramekins. Remove the foil and invert the ramekins onto plates to release the cakes. Dust with confectioners' sugar and serve warm.

VARIATION TIP: Try topping your mini soufflés with melted peanut butter. It's a match made in heaven.

Per Serving: Calories: 441; Carbohydrates: 53g; Fat: 21g; Fiber: 3g; Protein: 8g; Sugar: 43g; Sodium: 63mg

Desserts

CHAPTER

SAUCES AND STAPLES

CHICKEN BROTH

Serves 2

PREP & FINISHING: 10 minutes   **PRESSURE COOK:** 45 minutes on High
PRESSURE RELEASE: Natural for 30 minutes, then Quick   **TOTAL TIME:** 1 hour 30 minutes

Chicken broth always comes in handy, especially when you cook with your Instant Pot often. So if you have leftover chicken bones, grab some vegetable scraps and use this simple recipe to whip up more amazing meals.

1 chicken carcass or bones from whole chicken

1 cup vegetable scraps (such as carrot peels, onions, celery)

1 thyme sprig

1 bay leaf

1½ teaspoons salt

½ teaspoon black pepper

5 cups cold water

1. Combine the chicken bones, vegetable scraps, thyme, bay leaf, salt, and pepper in the Instant Pot, then pour in the water.

2. Lock the lid in place. Select Pressure Cook and adjust the pressure to High and the time to 45 minutes. After cooking, let the pressure release naturally for 30 minutes, then quick release any remaining pressure.

3. Once the float valve drops, open the lid. Strain the broth and allow it to cool slightly, then transfer to an airtight container and store in the refrigerator for up to 4 days or in the freezer for up to 6 months.

VARIATION TIP: Increase the cook time to 2 hours for nutrient-dense bone broth.

Per Serving (1 cup): Calories: 20; Carbohydrates: 2g; Fat: 0g; Fiber: 0g; Protein: 2g; Sugar: 0g; Sodium: 436mg

HARD-BOILED EGGS

Serves 2
PREP & FINISHING: 5 minutes   **PRESSURE COOK:** 5 minutes on High
PRESSURE RELEASE: Natural for 5 minutes, then Quick   **TOTAL TIME:** 15 minutes

---

Hard-boiled eggs are perfect sliced and served on toast for breakfast, as an easy snack eaten whole with a sprinkle of salt, or chopped on salads or veggie bowls for added protein. Make these perfect, no-fuss eggs in your Instant Pot in just minutes.

4 large eggs

1. Place a trivet in the bottom of the Instant Pot, then pour in 1 cup water.

2. Place the whole eggs on the trivet.

3. Lock the lid in place. Select Pressure Cook and adjust the pressure to High and the time to 5 minutes. After cooking, let the pressure release naturally for 5 minutes, then quick release any remaining pressure.

4. Once the float valve drops, open the lid and transfer the eggs to a bowl of ice-cold water.

5. Once cool, peel the eggs to enjoy right away or store unpeeled in an airtight container in the refrigerator for up to 1 week.

> **VARIATION TIP:** For soft-boiled eggs, adjust the cook time to 3 minutes on Low pressure and quick release after cooking.

Per Serving: Calories: 143; Carbohydrates: 1g; Fat: 10g; Fiber: 0g; Protein: 13g; Sugar: 0g; Sodium: 142mg

Sauces and Staples

117

MARINARA SAUCE

Serves 2

PREP & FINISHING: 10 minutes   **PRESSURE COOK:** 25 minutes on High
PRESSURE RELEASE: Natural for 10 minutes, then Quick   **TOTAL TIME:** 50 minutes

Don't have any jars of pasta sauce on hand? No problem! Make this basic marinara sauce in the Instant Pot using a few pantry staples for healthier, more flavorful pasta dishes.

1 (14.5-ounce) can whole peeled tomatoes

2 teaspoons minced garlic

½ onion, quartered

1 teaspoon Italian seasoning

1 tablespoon tomato paste

1. Combine the tomatoes with their juices, garlic, onion, and Italian seasoning in the Instant Pot. Add the tomato paste last, but do not stir.

2. Lock the lid in place. Select Pressure Cook and adjust the pressure to High and the time to 25 minutes. After cooking, let the pressure release naturally for 10 minutes, then quick release any remaining pressure.

3. Once the float valve drops, open the lid. Remove the onion pieces and discard. Using a potato masher or immersion blender, blend to your desired consistency and serve warm.

VARIATION TIP: Spice things up with a pinch or two of red pepper flakes during the cooking process.

Per Serving: Calories: 55; Carbohydrates: 12g; Fat: 1g; Fiber: 5g; Protein: 2g; Sugar: 7g; Sodium: 243mg

SALSA

Serves 2

PREP & FINISHING: 10 minutes   **PRESSURE COOK:** 5 minutes on High
PRESSURE RELEASE: Natural for 10 minutes, then Quick
TOTAL TIME: 30 minutes, plus chilling time

Chips and salsa is one of my all-time favorite snacks. So naturally, I had to figure out how to create restaurant-style salsa at home. I love that this recipe is packed full of fresh ingredients for a flavorful sauce to go with your favorite chips or top your Chicken Tacos (page 71).

5 Roma tomatoes

1 sweet onion, chopped

1 green bell pepper, seeded and chopped

2 teaspoons minced garlic

1 tablespoon lime juice

¼ teaspoon salt

Chopped fresh cilantro (optional)

1. Put the tomatoes in the Instant Pot and gently smash them until the skin breaks and the juices come out.

2. Add the onion, bell pepper, and garlic, and stir.

3. Lock the lid in place. Select Pressure Cook and adjust the pressure to High and the time to 5 minutes. After cooking, let the pressure release naturally for 10 minutes, then quick release any remaining pressure.

4. Once the float valve drops, open the lid. Using an immersion blender, blend to your desired consistency.

5. Stir in the lime juice, salt, and cilantro (if using). Cover and chill in the refrigerator for at least 1 hour before serving.

VARIATION TIP: Spice things up by adding jalapeños to the mix. The amount will vary depending on your desired level of heat; start with 1 or 2 peppers, seeded and chopped, added at the same time as the onion, bell pepper, and garlic.

Per Serving: Calories: 182; Carbohydrates: 41g; Fat: 1g; Fiber: 10g; Protein: 7g; Sugar: 26g; Sodium: 337mg

Sauces and Staples

119

WHITE RICE

Serves 2

PREP & FINISHING: 5 minutes   **PRESSURE COOK:** 4 minutes on High
PRESSURE RELEASE: Natural for 15 minutes, then Quick   **TOTAL TIME:** 29 minutes

Kick that rice maker to the curb—the Instant Pot makes fluffy, perfectly cooked rice in just minutes. Plus, this smaller-batch recipe will ensure you eat all the rice you made.

1 cup white rice

1 cup water

¼ teaspoon salt (optional)

1. Combine the rice, water, and salt (if desired) in the Instant Pot.

2. Lock the lid in place. Select Pressure Cook and adjust the pressure to High and the time to 4 minutes. After cooking, let the pressure release naturally for 15 minutes, then quick release any remaining pressure.

3. Once the float valve drops, open the lid. Fluff the rice with a fork and serve warm.

VARIATION TIP: For a hint of sweetness, swap out ¾ cup of the water for a 13.5-ounce can of coconut milk.

Per Serving: Calories: 351; Carbohydrates: 77g; Fat: 1g; Fiber: 1g; Protein: 6g; Sugar: 0g; Sodium: 1mg

SPICED BLACK BEANS

Serves 2

PREP & FINISHING: 10 minutes   **PRESSURE COOK:** 25 minutes on High
PRESSURE RELEASE: Natural for 15 minutes, then Quick   **TOTAL TIME:** 55 minutes

Black beans are the perfect pantry staple to keep on hand. They're perfect as a side dish or added to meals like Quinoa Stuffed Peppers (page 58) and Veggie Burritos (page 62).

1 cup dried black beans	¼ teaspoon ground cumin	1½ cups water
½ onion, chopped	¼ teaspoon chili powder	½ teaspoon salt
2 teaspoons minced garlic	⅛ teaspoon black pepper	

1. Combine the black beans, onion, garlic, cumin, chili powder, and pepper in the Instant Pot. Pour in the water and stir.

2. Lock the lid in place. Select Pressure Cook and adjust the pressure to High and the time to 25 minutes. After cooking, let the pressure release naturally for 15 minutes, then quick release any remaining pressure.

3. Once the float valve drops, open the lid. Stir in the salt and serve warm.

VARIATION TIP: Add a jalapeño pepper, seeded and chopped, for a little heat.

Per Serving: Calories: 347; Carbohydrates: 64g; Fat: 1g; Fiber: 16g; Protein: 21g; Sugar: 3g; Sodium: 598mg

Sauces and Staples

APPLESAUCE

Serves 2

PREP & FINISHING: 15 minutes   **PRESSURE COOK:** 5 minutes on High
PRESSURE RELEASE: Natural for 20 minutes, then Quick   **TOTAL TIME:** 45 minutes

You haven't had applesauce until you've had homemade applesauce. And this recipe is a great way to use apples you have sitting around, plus just a little lemon juice and cinnamon—and a little added sweetness if you like.

2 large sweet apples (such as Honeycrisp or Gala), peeled, cored, and chopped

2 large tart apples (such as Granny Smith or Golden Delicious), peeled, cored, and chopped

½ cup water

1 tablespoon lemon juice

½ teaspoon ground cinnamon

2 tablespoons packed light brown sugar (optional)

1. Combine the apples, water, lemon juice, and cinnamon in the Instant Pot and stir well to coat.

2. Lock the lid in place. Select Pressure Cook and adjust the pressure to High and the time to 5 minutes. After cooking, let the pressure release naturally for 20 minutes, then quick release any remaining pressure.

3. Once the float valve drops, open the lid. Add the brown sugar (if using) and use a potato masher or an immersion blender to blend to your desired consistency.

4. Enjoy immediately or transfer to jars to store in the refrigerator for up to 1 week.

SUBSTITUTION TIP: Skip the brown sugar and sweeten the applesauce with maple syrup or honey instead.

Per Serving: Calories: 211; Carbohydrates: 56g; Fat: 1g; Fiber: 6g; Protein: 1g; Sugar: 44g; Sodium: 0mg

Sauces and Staples

REFRIED BEANS

Serves 2

PREP & FINISHING: 10 minutes   **PRESSURE COOK:** 20 minutes on High

PRESSURE RELEASE: Natural for 10 minutes, then Quick   **TOTAL TIME:** 45 minutes

No soaking required! The perfect addition to tacos, enchiladas, and more, refried beans come together easily in the Instant Pot, without skimping on the homemade taste.

1 cup dried pinto beans	3 cups water	½ teaspoon salt
½ onion, chopped	1 teaspoon ground cumin	¼ teaspoon black pepper
2 teaspoons minced garlic	1 teaspoon chili powder	

1. Combine the pinto beans, onion, and garlic in the Instant Pot. Pour in the water and stir.

2. Lock the lid in place. Select Pressure Cook and adjust the pressure to High and the time to 20 minutes. After cooking, let the pressure release naturally for 10 minutes, then quick release any remaining pressure.

3. Once the float valve drops, open the lid. Drain the beans in a strainer set over a bowl, reserving the cooking liquid.

4. Return the beans to the inner pot and stir in ½ cup of the reserved cooking liquid, along with the cumin, chili powder, salt, and pepper.

5. Using a potato masher or immersion blender, blend to your desired consistency. Serve warm.

SUBSTITUTION TIP: Try replacing the water with the same amount of chicken broth for added flavor.

Per Serving: Calories: 354; Carbohydrates: 64g; Fat: 1g; Fiber: 16g; Protein: 22g; Sugar: 3g; Sodium: 633mg

STRAWBERRY JAM

Serves 2

PREP & FINISHING: 40 minutes   **PRESSURE COOK:** 1 minute on High
PRESSURE RELEASE: Natural for 15 minutes, then Quick   **SAUTÉ:** 8 minutes
TOTAL TIME: 1 hour 9 minutes

Who needs store-bought jam when you can make this delicious, homemade version in the Instant Pot? Only three ingredients are needed to make this sweet and tasty spread.

2 cups strawberries, hulled and quartered	½ cup sugar	2 tablespoons lemon juice

1. Combine the strawberries, sugar, and lemon juice in the Instant Pot.

2. Close the lid and let them sit for 30 minutes, then open the lid and stir the strawberries.

3. Lock the lid in place. Select Pressure Cook and adjust the pressure to High and the time to 1 minute. After cooking, let the pressure release naturally for 15 minutes, then quick release any remaining pressure.

4. Once the float valve drops, open the lid. Press Cancel to turn off the Instant Pot.

5. Using a potato masher or immersion blender, blend the jam to your desired consistency.

6. Set the Instant Pot to Sauté and let the mixture come to a boil. Let boil for 5 minutes, stirring frequently, until the jam thickens. Press Cancel to turn off the Instant Pot.

7. Let the jam cool, then transfer to a jar and store in the refrigerator for up to 1 month.

VARIATION TIP: Toss in a little grated lemon zest during the cooking process for even more flavor.

Per Serving: Calories: 245; Carbohydrates: 63g; Fat: 0g; Fiber: 3g; Protein: 1g; Sugar: 58g; Sodium: 2mg

Sauces and Staples

DULCE DE LECHE

Serves 2

PREP & FINISHING: 5 minutes   **PRESSURE COOK:** 35 minutes on High
PRESSURE RELEASE: Quick   **TOTAL TIME:** 45 minutes

Whether you drizzle it on desserts, dip fruit into it, or stir a spoonful into your coffee, dulce de leche is one decadent treat you want to know how to make. The Instant Pot makes it a breeze to have your favorite caramel sauce on hand in no time.

1 (14-ounce) can sweet-ened condensed milk

1 teaspoon pure vanilla extract

1. Open the can of sweetened condensed milk and remove the paper label. Cover and wrap the entire can tightly with aluminum foil.

2. Place a trivet in the Instant Pot and place the can on the trivet.

3. Pour enough water into the inner pot until the can is submerged halfway (about 5 cups for a 3-quart Instant Pot or 10 cups for a 6- or 8-quart Instant Pot).

4. Lock the lid in place. Select Pressure Cook and adjust the pressure to High and the time to 35 minutes. After cooking, move the steam release handle to venting and quick release the pressure.

5. Once the float valve drops, open the lid and carefully remove the can.

6. Pour the hot dulce de leche into a small bowl and whisk in the vanilla until smooth.

7. Serve warm; refrigerate leftover dulce de leche in a covered jar for up to 2 weeks.

VARIATION TIP: Looking for a darker caramel hue? Stir ¼ teaspoon of baking soda into the can of sweetened condensed milk before cooking.

Per Serving: Calories: 864; Carbohydrates: 146g; Fat: 23g; Fiber: 0g; Protein: 21g; Sugar: 146g; Sodium: 340mg

Measurement Conversions

VOLUME EQUIVALENTS	U.S. STANDARD	U.S. STANDARD (OUNCES)	METRIC (APPROXIMATE)
LIQUID	2 tablespoons	1 fl. oz.	30 mL
	¼ cup	2 fl. oz.	60 mL
	½ cup	4 fl. oz.	120 mL
	1 cup	8 fl. oz.	240 mL
	1½ cups	12 fl. oz.	355 mL
	2 cups or 1 pint	16 fl. oz.	475 mL
	4 cups or 1 quart	32 fl. oz.	1 L
	1 gallon	128 fl. oz.	4 L
DRY	⅛ teaspoon	—	0.5 mL
	¼ teaspoon	—	1 mL
	½ teaspoon	—	2 mL
	¾ teaspoon	—	4 mL
	1 teaspoon	—	5 mL
	1 tablespoon	—	15 mL
	¼ cup	—	59 mL
	⅓ cup	—	79 mL
	½ cup	—	118 mL
	⅔ cup	—	156 mL
	¾ cup	—	177 mL
	1 cup	—	235 mL
	2 cups or 1 pint	—	475 mL
	3 cups	—	700 mL
	4 cups or 1 quart	—	1 L
	½ gallon	—	2 L
	1 gallon	—	4 L

OVEN TEMPERATURES

FAHRENHEIT	CELSIUS (APPROXIMATE)
250°F	120°C
300°F	150°C
325°F	165°C
350°F	180°C
375°F	190°C
400°F	200°C
425°F	220°C
450°F	230°C

WEIGHT EQUIVALENTS

U.S. STANDARD	METRIC (APPROXIMATE)
½ ounce	15 g
1 ounce	30 g
2 ounces	60 g
4 ounces	115 g
8 ounces	225 g
12 ounces	340 g
16 ounces or 1 pound	455 g

Instant Pot Pressure Cooking Time Charts

FISH AND SEAFOOD

All times are for steamed fish and shellfish.

	MINUTES UNDER PRESSURE	PRESSURE	RELEASE
Clams	2	High	Quick
Halibut (1 inch thick)	3	High	Quick
Mussels	1	High	Quick
Salmon (1 inch thick)	5	Low	Quick
Shrimp, large (frozen)	1	Low	Quick
Tilapia or cod (frozen)	3	Low	Quick

POULTRY

Except as noted, these times are for braised poultry; that is, partially submerged in liquid.

	MINUTES UNDER PRESSURE	PRESSURE	RELEASE
Chicken breast, bone-in	8 (steamed)	Low	Natural 5 minutes, then Quick
Chicken breast, boneless	5 (steamed)	Low	Natural 8 minutes, then Quick
Chicken thigh, bone-in	12 to 15	High	Natural 10 minutes, then Quick
Chicken thigh, boneless, whole	8	High	Natural 10 minutes, then Quick
Chicken thigh, 1- to 2-inch pieces	5 to 6	High	Quick
Chicken, whole (seared on all sides)	14 to 18	Low	Natural 8 minutes, then Quick
Duck quarters, bone-in	35	High	Quick
Turkey breast, tenderloin (12 ounces)	5 (steamed)	Low	Natural 8 minutes, then Quick
Turkey thigh, bone-in	30	High	Natural

MEAT

Except as noted, these times are for braised meats; that is, meats that are seared before pressure cooking, and partially submerged in liquid.

	MINUTES UNDER PRESSURE	PRESSURE	RELEASE
Beef, shoulder (chuck) roast (2 pounds)	35 to 45	High	Natural
Beef, shoulder (chuck), 2-inch chunks	20	High	Natural 10 minutes, then Quick
Beef, bone-in short ribs	40	High	Natural
Beef, flat-iron steak, cut into ½-inch strips	6	Low	Quick
Beef, sirloin steak, cut into ½-inch strips	3	Low	Quick
Lamb, shanks	40	High	Natural
Lamb, shoulder, 2-inch chunks	35	High	Natural
Pork back ribs (steamed)	25	High	Quick
Pork spare ribs (steamed)	20	High	Quick
Pork shoulder roast (2 pounds)	25	High	Natural
Pork, shoulder, 2-inch chunks	20	High	Quick
Pork tenderloin	4	Low	Quick
Smoked pork sausage, ½-inch slices	5 to 10	High	Quick

BEANS AND LEGUMES

When cooking beans, if you have a pound or more, it's best to use low pressure and increase the cooking time by a minute or two (with larger amounts, there's more chance of foaming at high pressure). If you have less than a pound, high pressure is fine. A little oil in the cooking liquid will reduce foaming. Where two times are listed, the shorter time is for high pressure and the longer time for low pressure.

	MINUTES UNDER PRESSURE	PRESSURE	RELEASE
Black beans	8 or 9	Low or High	Natural
Black-eyed peas	5	High	Natural 8 minutes, then Quick
Cannellini beans	5 or 7	Low or High	Natural
Chickpeas (garbanzo beans)	4	High	Natural 3 minutes, then Quick
Kidney beans	5 to 7	Low or High	Natural
Lentils, brown (unsoaked)	20	High	Natural 10 minutes, then Quick
Lentils, red (unsoaked)	10	High	Natural 5 minutes, then Quick
Lima beans	4 to 5	Low or High	Natural 5 minutes, then Quick
Pinto beans	8 or 10	Low or High	Natural
Soybeans, dried	12 or 14	Low or High	Natural
Soybeans, fresh (edamame), unsoaked	1	High	Quick
Split peas (unsoaked)	5 to 8	Low or High	Natural

GRAINS

To prevent foaming, it's best to include a small amount of butter or oil with the cooking liquid for these grains or to rinse them thoroughly before cooking.

	LIQUID PER 1 CUP OF GRAIN	MINUTES UNDER PRESSURE	PRESSURE	RELEASE
Arborio (or other medium-grain) rice	1½ cups	6 to 20 (depending on use)	High	Quick
Barley, pearled	2½ cups	20	High	Natural 10 minutes, then Quick
Brown rice, long-grain	1½ cups	13	High	Natural 10 minutes, then Quick
Brown rice, medium-grain	1½ cups	6 to 8	High	Natural
Buckwheat	1¾ cups	2 to 4	High	Natural
Farro, pearled	2 cups	6 to 8	High	Natural
Farro, whole-grain	3 cups	22 to 24	High	Natural
Oats, rolled	3 cups	3 to 4	High	Quick
Oats, steel-cut	4 cups	12	High	Natural
Quinoa	1½ cups	1	High	Natural 12 minutes, then Quick
Wheat berries	2 cups	30	High	Natural 10 minutes, then Quick
Long-grain white rice	1 cup	3	High	Natural
Wild rice	1¼ cups	22 to 24	High	Natural

VEGETABLES

The cooking method for the following vegetables is steaming; if the vegetables are cooked in liquid, the times may vary. Green vegetables will be tender-crisp; root vegetables will be soft.

	PREP	MINUTES UNDER PRESSURE	PRESSURE	RELEASE
Acorn squash	Halved	9	High	Quick
Artichokes, large	Whole	15	High	Quick
Beets	Quartered if large; halved if small	9	High	Natural
Broccoli	Cut into florets	1	Low	Quick
Brussels sprouts	Halved	2	High	Quick
Butternut squash	Peeled, cut into ½-inch chunks	8	High	Quick
Cabbage	Sliced	5	High	Quick
Carrots	Sliced	5	High	Quick
Cauliflower	Whole	6	High	Quick
Cauliflower	Cut into florets	1	Low	Quick
Green beans	Cut in half or thirds	1	Low	Quick
Potatoes, large russet	Quartered; for mashing	8	High	Natural 8 minutes, then Quick
Potatoes, red	Whole if less than 1½ inch across; halved if larger	4	High	Quick
Spaghetti squash	Halved lengthwise	7	High	Quick
Sweet potatoes	Halved lengthwise	8	High	Natural

Index

ACKNOWLEDGMENTS

There are so many people I'd like to thank for making this cookbook possible. First, thank you to my husband, Andre, who always supports me and encouraged me to write this cookbook. Thank you to my boys, AJ, Alex, and Adrian, for being my inspiration and the best taste-testers.

Thank you to my mom, Reba, who was so excited from the start and made the best sous-chef while we created so many recipes. I couldn't have done this without you and will always remember the time we spent in the kitchen together.

Thank you to my family and friends Mary, Jon, Janice, Rebecca, Melissa, and Parisa, who all inspired recipes in this book. The meals you create for your family are always delicious and filled with love.

ABOUT THE AUTHOR

KIMBERLY SNEED is the creator of the popular blog *A Night Owl*. She grew up in a home where her mother loved cooking, so she understands the value of gathering around good food and the love that it can bring. Now she loves to create simple and easy meals for her family. She has been sharing easy recipes online for more than 10 years and treasures the community of followers and friends that she has established. Kimberly truly feels that food brings everyone together and that great food creates moments to be remembered.